Mobile Interactions in Context

A Designerly Way Toward Digital Ecology

Synthesis Lectures on Human-Centered Informatics

Editor
John M. Carroll, *Penn State University*

Human-Centered Informatics (HCI) is the intersection of the cultural, the social, the cognitive, and the aesthetic with computing and information technology. It encompasses a huge range of issues, theories, technologies, designs, tools, environments and human experiences in knowledge work, recreation and leisure activity, teaching and learning, and the potpourri of everyday life. The series will publish state-of-the-art syntheses, case studies, and tutorials in key areas. It will share the focus of leading international conferences in HCI.

Context-Aware Mobile Computing: Affordances of Space, Social Awareness, and Social Influence
Geri Gay
2009

Studies of Work and the Workplace in HCI: Concepts and Techniques
Graham Button, Wes Sharrock
2009

Semiotic Engineering Methods for Scientific Research in HCI
Clarisse Sieckenius de Souza, Carla Faria Leitão
2009

Common Ground in Electronically Mediated Conversation
Andrew Monk
2008

Mobile Interactions in Context: A Designerly Way Toward Digital Ecology
Jesper Kjeldskov

ISBN: 978-3-031-01076-7 print
ISBN: 978-3-031-02204-3 ebook

DOI 10.1007/978-3-031-02204-3

A Publication in the Springer series
SYNTHESIS LECTURES ON HUMAN-CENTERED INFORMATICS #21
Series Editor: John M. Carroll, Penn State University

Series ISSN   1946-7680 Print   1946-7699 Electronic

Figure 5.1: from Alexander, C. *The Nature of Order*. Vol. 2: The Process of Creating Life. Copyright © 2002, Center for Environmental Structure Publishing. Used with permission.

Mobile Interactions in Context

A Designerly Way Toward Digital Ecology

Jesper Kjeldskov
Aalborg University

SYNTHESIS LECTURES ON HUMAN-CENTERED INFORMATICS #21

ABSTRACT

Imagination is more important than knowledge. For knowledge is limited, whereas imagination embraces the entire world
— Albert Einstein

This book presents a contextual approach to designing contemporary interactive mobile computer systems as integral parts of ubiquitous computing environments. Interactive mobile systems, services, and devices have become functional design objects that we care deeply about. Although their look, feel, and features impact our everyday lives as we orchestrate them in concert with a plethora of other computing technologies, these artifacts are not well understood or created through traditional methods of user-centered design and usability engineering. Contrary to more traditional IT artifacts, they constitute holistic user experiences of value and pleasure that require careful attention to the variety, complexity, and dynamics of their usage. Hence, the design of mobile interactions proposed in this book transcends existing approaches by using the ensemble of form and context as its central unit of analysis. As such, it promotes a designerly way of achieving convergence between form and context through a contextually grounded, wholeness sensitive, and continually unfolding process of design.

KEYWORDS

mobile, interaction design, form, context, designerly thinking, wholeness extending, digital ecosystems

Contents

In memory of Steve Howard, friend and mentor

Preface

At the end of 2010, for the first time, more smartphones were being sold worldwide than personal computers, hailing the coming of the "post-PC" era. This enormous uptake of mobile computers has had a huge impact on the way we perceive and use these technologies in our work and private lives. Interactive mobile systems and devices have become functional design objects that we care deeply about the look, feel, and experience of, and that we orchestrate in concert with a plethora of other computing technologies in our everyday lives. If such systems and devices are to be successful, they need to be designed to fit into the greater whole, or digital ecosystem, of other devices, systems, and services that are part of the contextual richness of the world around us. This is not achieved well through traditional methods of user-centered design and usability engineering. Instead, I argue that it calls for designerly approaches to interaction design that help us create desired practice, design for wholes rather than focusing on the parts, and deal with the often ill-defined and changing goals emerging from the process.

As a particularly important source of inspiration for developing such approaches to interaction design, I have always been fascinated by thoughts and practices in the discipline of architecture, especially the practice of embracing a contextual approach. The relationship between interaction design and architecture has been addressed previously by others, but, in my opinion, there is still much to be learned from architectural design on how to think about and do interaction design. Looking at the design of mobile interactions as a continual convergence of form and context is an attempt to provide this designerly approach to thinking and doing interaction design, inspired by thoughts and practices in architecture. Through this approach, I seek to explore the view that most activities are unbounded and situated in dynamic contexts, and that the relationship between context and form is therefore a continually changing one—requiring that design is inherently cyclic, able to deal with emergent and changing goals, and about construction of context as well as form.

This book represents the essence of my recent dissertation for the degree of Doctor of Science (higher doctorate) awarded from Aalborg University in 2013. The dissertation consisted of a longer version of the present manuscript accompanied by 23 selected publications from my research on mobile interaction design between 2001 and 2012. By condensing this work into a shorter format, I am hoping to reach a broader audience of interaction design researchers and practitioners.

My research interest in mobile interaction design began around 2000 when I first started working with application design for the PalmPilot and the potentials of Internet access on mobile devices. Looking for inspiration, I attended the Mobile HCI 2001 workshop in Lille, France. Back then this was a small 1-day meeting, but it was so inspirational that I immediately began writing on a submission for the next year's event. The resulting paper on "just-in-place Information" became my first publication on mobile interaction design, and its notion of "indexical interaction design" set the foundation for my future collaboration with Steve Howard and Frank Vetere's group at The University of Melbourne, where I was fortunate enough to spend a lot of time over the years that followed. It was during this time that I met Connor Graham, and we compiled our Mobile HCI research methods survey article for the Mobile HCI 2003 conference, and my Danish colleague Mikael B. Skov, and I asked if it was "worth the hassle" to investigate mobile usability in the field. It was also in Australia that I met and worked with Kenton O'Hara on "blended interaction spaces," leading to new levels of depth and inspiration. And, of course, it was in Melbourne that I met my Australian wife, the lovely Jeni Paay.

Over the years, I have worked particularly closely with Steve, Frank, Mikael, Jeni, and Kenton. Together with Steve and Frank I investigated the use of mobile technologies for mediating close personal relationships (over several bottles of red wine). Mikael and I went from working with evaluation techniques to focusing more on interaction design and studying the broader use of mobile and pervasive technologies in various domestic settings (over several bottles of beer). Together with Jeni, I developed the concept of indexical interaction design further, and began exploring the use of sketching and other general design techniques in mobile interaction design, drawing on her background in architecture, (over several bottles of champagne). Kenton and I took on big challenges and won. These collaborations have all been essential for the thinking presented in this book. It was, however, when Steve spent 6 months in Aalborg in 2005–2006, that the ideas for my Doctor of Science dissertation were formed. Steve and I discussed the need for interaction design research to cast a wider perspective on the orchestration of multiple devices, rather than looking at interactions with individual artifacts, and we discussed alternative approaches to traditional user-centred design for doing this.

Most of my research was developed and carried out at the Department of Computer Science at Aalborg University and the Department of Information Systems at The University of Melbourne, and was funded by the Danish Technical Research Council, The Obel Family Foundation, and Aalborg University's Faculty of Engineering and Science and Department of Computer Science. I wish to thank these institutions for their support and, in particular, thank my primary collaborators and co-authors over the last decade: Jeni Paay, Mikael B. Skov, Steve Howard, Frank Vetere, Connor Graham, Kenton O'Hara, Jon Pearce, and Jan Stage. Very special thanks to Yvonne Rogers, Susanne Bødker, Peter Axel Nielsen, Lars Mathiassen, Steve Howard, Erik Frøkjær, Jeni Paay, Mikael B. Skov, Ivan Aaen, Matt Jones, and Jack Carroll for feedback on earlier drafts of the book and the preceding dissertation, and fruitful discussions of my work. Special thanks to Ellen Christiansen for introducing me to the works of Christopher Alexander, to Marianne Stokholm for engaging discussions on design methods from a designerly perspective, and to Diane Cerra and everyone at Morgan & Claypool Publishers. I also thank my colleagues at Aalborg University's Department of

Computer Science, especially the members of the Information Systems group/Centre for Socio+Interactive Design, and in particular Head of Department, Kristian G. Olesen, for providing the organizational support for this work. Finally, I wish to thank all my Masters and Ph.D. students in Human-Computer Interaction over the years who have contributed to my work through prototype experiments, user experience studies, and discussions on mobile interaction design. In particular, Dimitrios Raptis, Henrik Sørensen, Jacob H. Smedegård, and Rahuvaran Pathmanathan,

Finally, I thank my wife Jeni for giving me the space needed for thinking and writing.

Jesper Kjeldskov
July 2014

Introduction

"Imagination is more important than knowledge. For knowledge is limited, whereas imagination embraces the entire world" (Einstein 1931). In computing and interaction design today, imagination is every bit as important to advance our knowledge and practices as it was to science in the 1930's. Without imagination and creativity we are not able to move beyond how we think and do today, toward the thinking and doing of tomorrow. This is the timeless way of designing, and it is my starting point for looking at the design of mobile interactions. How can we imagine thinking and acting differently in order to enable ourselves to make future generations of interactive computer systems and devices fundamentally better than the ones we have now? Our current landscape of interactive technologies has itself grown out of paradigmatic shifts in the way we thought about computer systems and did systems development in the past. These shifts brought computing into areas like the workplace, home office, and private sphere, and it made computing about things like work support, collaboration, communication, media consumption, and social networking. But where do we go from here? How can we, once again, reach beyond our presently established ways of thinking and doing, and actively advance the design of interactive computer systems of tomorrow? In this book I am going to address this question by revisiting my research contributions within the area of interaction design for mobile computer systems.

One of the things that makes mobile computing an interesting topic of research and design is that the area is strongly driven by innovation, characterized by rapidly evolving use, and has enormous market potential and growth. New technologies are constantly being developed, new use domains are constantly being explored, and successful new ideas and applications reach millions of users. In fact, by the end of 2010 more smartphones were, for the first time, being sold worldwide than personal computers, with more than 100 million units shipped in the last 3 months of that year alone. Reflecting this dynamic and rapidly evolving nature of the area, the industrial lead position has been passed on several times within only a decade, from Palm to Nokia to Apple, and is most likely to be passed on again in the future. This obviously motivates researchers and designers to keep innovating and developing new technology and applications. A primary driver of mobile technology development has been the enormous uptake of interactive systems and devices for work as well as for leisure. Mobile phones have long been something almost everyone owns at least one of and uses extensively for personal purposes and not just for work. With Internet and multimedia-enabled phones such as the Apple iPhone, smart phones have now firmly reached this mass market too and are no longer something exclusively for a small elite of business professionals. The uptake of mobile technology in our work and private spheres has had a huge impact on the way we perceive and use these technologies. They are no longer just computers on batteries. They have become functional design objects, which we care deeply about the look, feel, and experience of, and that we juggle in multitude in our everyday lives. Hence, work in the area of mobile computing has rapidly evolved from being strongly an *engineering* profession to being, at least, equally strongly a *design* profession where the contextual user experience of interactive mobile systems and devices, and the digital ecosystems they are forming, is of utmost importance. This presents the field of mobile interaction design with new challenges forcing us to seek beyond traditional approaches of user- or technology-centeredness.

Being a design profession is different from being an engineering profession. It involves careful engineering, but where engineering is about implementing a solid solution to a problem, design is about also understanding and defining that problem in the first place, and exploring a wide range of solutions before choosing which one to implement. This requires different methods and techniques than the ones taught at engineering schools. It requires techniques that sit at the intersection between technology and user experience design—that support the process of exploring a problem and a design space by generating, communicating and reflecting on ideas, and facilitate choosing between multiple paths of possible solutions. Traditional usability engineering and user-centered design approaches do not facilitate such opportunity seeking ideation and elaboration, but are better at supporting decision making for further reduction and specification of a particular solution.

Mobile computing is a relatively new field of research with little more than three decades of history. During its lifetime it has expanded from being primarily technical to now also being about usability, usefulness and user experiences. This has led to the birth of the vibrant area of *mobile interaction design* at the intersections between, among others, mobile computing, social sciences, human-computer interaction, industrial design, and user experience design. However, the field of mobile interaction design is still young and immature. Growing out of the "Mobile HCI" community of the early 2000's, it has survived infancy and become an acknowledged part of the established research area of computing with a notable presence in mainstream HCI literature and with its own conferences and journals. But it still doesn't have a strong and unified identity. There is no well-defined methodological and theoretical base for the design of mobile interactions, or even a catalog of best practices, and there are no well-defined goals or benchmarks for good mobile interaction design research. This is not to say that there is not a lot of good mobile interaction design and research taking place. There is indeed. It is, however, rather fragmented, and rather than an organized community the research field can better be characterized as "being composed of a number of roving tribes who occasionally encounter one another, warily engage, and, finding the engagements stimulating, remain open to other encounters" (Erickson 2006, p. 301). The advantage of this might be a high level of autonomy, but the disadvantage is less than optimal collective accumulation of knowledge and impeding our ability to leap forward in a pace beyond small incremental steps of each individual piece of research.

This book is an attempt to respond to these new challenges by suggesting a holistic approach that rethinks and ties together central activities of interaction design into an ongoing process revolving around the central concept of converging form and context. By convergence I simply mean the combination of two or more things that in concert make up something new that is bigger than the sum of the contributing parts. In my understanding of form and context I subscribe to the fundamental view promoted by Christopher Alexander in his 1964 "Notes on the Synthesis of Form." According to Alexander, design is "an effort to achieve fitness between two entities: the form in question and its context" (Alexander 1964, p. 15). "Form" is the response to a situation, or problem, whereas "context" defines or frames this situation or problem. In this use of the term, form does not just mean physical shape, but unites *shape*, *look*, *function*, and *content*. Using this conceptual optic the design of mobile interactions is about considering the ensemble of particular forms (i.e., interactive mobile systems) in relation to their context (i.e., users, technology, settings, activities, etc.).

Figure I.1: Form and context in the design of mobile interactions.

Following Alexander's line of thought, when we deal with the process of design "the real object of discussion is not the form alone, but the *ensemble* comprising the form and its context" (Alexander 1964, p. 16, italics added). Hence, the quality of a designed form-context ensemble as a whole can change *either* by changing the form *or* by changes in the context. In response to this, the views promoted in this book build on the belief that the design of mobile interactions should embrace the potentials of designing for wholes, rather than individual parts, and that the notion of form-context ensembles provides a suitable higher-level unit of analysis for such change in focus and scope.

The work presented in this book aspires to contribute to the accumulation of a theoretical and methodological body of knowledge about mobile interaction design. It is grounded in my research on interaction design for mobile systems and devices, and uses this foundation to shape a holistic perspective on the process of mobile interaction design in which the main activities of studying, analyzing, designing, and building interactive mobile systems revolves around the central unity of form-context convergence.

Chapter 2 traces the history of mobile computing through seven distinct phases, and introduces the discipline of interaction design. This is followed, in Chapter 3, by a description of the most notable existing design approaches within the field of interaction design. Chapter 4 describes the starting point for my own research on the design of mobile interactions in the early 2000's and outlines some of the emerging challenges facing us today. In response to these challenges, Chapter 5 discusses the need for doing, and thinking about, interaction design in a *designerly way* rather than in a traditional scientific way. This is followed by a critical discussion of the established user-centered design model in Chapter 6, leading to a series of proposed changes. Chapter 7 then presents and discusses, as an alternative, the design of mobile interactions as a matter of continual convergence of form and context. Finally, Chapter 8 summarizes the main points of observation made, addresses some potential challenges and limitations of a contextual approach to design, and puts forward some thoughts about where we can go from here.

CHAPTER 1

Mobile Computing

To ground my work on the design of mobile interactions I will first briefly trace the history of mobile computing. The purpose of this is to map out the origins of this field of research and design, show how it is continually evolving, and illustrate the influence of careful and innovative mobile interaction design at different points in time. This is followed by an introduction to the discipline of interaction design and its established design approaches.

Mobile computing is a significant contributor to the pervasiveness of computing resources in modern western civilisation. In concert with the proliferation of stationary and embedded computer technology throughout society, mobile devices, such as cell phones and other handheld or wearable computing technologies, have created a state of ubiquitous and pervasive computing where we are surrounded by more computational devices than people (Weiser 1991). Enabling us to orchestrate these devices to fit and serve our personal and working lives is a huge challenge for technology developers, and "as a consequence of pervasive computing, *interaction design* is poised to become one of the main liberal arts of the twenty-first century" (McCullough 2004, italics added).

The field of mobile computing has its origin in a fortunate alignment of interests by technologists and consumers. Since the dawn of the computing age there has always been technological aspirations to make computing hardware smaller, and ever since computers became widely accessible there has been a huge interest from consumers in being able to bring them with you (Atkinson 2005). As a result, the history of mobile computing is paved with countless commercially available devices. Most of them had short lifespan and minimal impact, but others significantly pushed the boundaries of engineering and interaction design. It is these devices, and their importance, that I wish to emphasize here.

The history of mobile computing can be divided into a number of eras, or waves, each characterized by a particular technological focus, interaction design trends, and by leading to fundamental changes in the design and use of mobile devices. In my view, the history of mobile computing has, so far, entailed seven particularly important waves. Although not strictly sequential, they provide a good overview of the legacy on which current mobile computing research and design is built.

1. Portability

2. Miniaturization

3. Connectivity

4. Convergence

5. Divergence

6. Apps

7. Digital ecosystems

The era of focus on *Portability* was about reducing the size of hardware to enable the creation of computers that could be physically moved around relatively easily. *Miniaturization* was about creating new and significantly smaller mobile form factors that allowed the use of personal mobile devices while on the move. *Connectivity* was about developing devices and applications that allowed users to be online and communicate via wireless data networks while on the move. *Convergence* was about integrating emerging types of digital mobile devices, such as PDAs, mobile phones, music players, cameras, games, etc., into hybrid devices. *Divergence* took an opposite approach to interaction design by promoting information appliances with specialized functionality rather than generalized ones. The latest wave of *apps* is about developing matter and substance for use and consumption on mobile devices, and making access to this fun or functional interactive application content easy and enjoyable. Finally, the emerging wave of *digital ecosystems* is about the larger wholes of pervasive and interrelated technologies that interactive mobile systems are increasingly becoming a part of.

1.1   PORTABILITY

The first mobile computers, the precursors to present time's laptops, were developed in the late 1970's and early 1980's inspired by the portability of Alan Kay's Dynabook concept from 1968 (Kay 1972). The Dynabook concept was originally thought of as a machine for children, but observant entrepreneurs, such as the founder of GRiD Systems, John Ellenby, quickly realized that the starting point for something that innovative would have to be "the customer with the most money and the most demanding need" (Moggridge 2007).

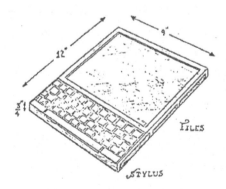

Figure 1.1: Alan Kay's Dynabook: "a personal computer for children of all ages" (Kay 1972).

The first laptop computer was the GRiD Compass 1101 designed by Bill Moggridge as early as 1981 in response to the design brief of fitting within half the space of a briefcase (Moggridge 2007; Atkinson 2005). The Compass had a 16 MHz Intel 8086 processor, 256 K DRAM, a 6-inch 320x240 pixel flat screen display, 340 kb bubble memory, a 1200 bit/s modem, weighed 5 kg, and ran its own graphical operating system called GRiD OS. It was primarily sold to the U.S. government and was, among others, used by NASA on Space Shuttle missions during the early 1980's, and in combat. The GRiD Compass featured a stunning forty-three innovative features in its utility patent, including the flat display and hinged screen. The first portable computer to reach real commercial success, however, was the suitcase-style Compaq Portable from 1982, which as the first official IBM clone could run MS-DOS and standard PC programs. In 1988, Grid Systems also developed the first tablet computer, the GRiDpad, initiated and led by Jeff Hawkins who later designed the first PalmPilot and founded Palm Computing.

GRiD Compass 1101 (1981)   Compaq Portable 1 (1982)   GRiDpad (1989)

Figure 1.2: Mobile computers in the 1980–1990's.

In terms of design longevity and impact, Bill Moggridge's work on the first laptop computer and Jeff Hawkins' work on the GRiDpad illustrates the value of careful and well-considered interaction design in mobile computing. The GRiD Compass was superior in terms of its design and performance for a decade. It defined the folding design still used in today's laptops 30 years later, and its basic form factor was not surpassed until the Apple PowerBook 100 introduced the, now standard, clamp-shell design and integrated pointing device in 1991. The basic design of the GRiDpad paved the way for tablet computers and handheld devices such as the Apple Newton, the PalmPilot, and even the iPad.

1.2   MINIATURIZATION

By the early 1990's the size of computer hardware had reached a point that allowed radically new and smaller form factors of mobile computers to evolve and emerge on the market. These predominantly handheld devices were labelled palmtop computers, digital organizers, or "Personal Digital

Assistants" (PDAs). PDAs differed from laptop PCs by being truly mobile and something that the users could operate while actually moving around physically. They were not thought of as alternatives to desktop or laptop computers but rather as small and lightweight supplemental devices for busy businessmen spending some of their time away from their PC. The first PDA was the Apple Newton in 1992. In 1997 the first PalmPilot was introduced, and in 2000 Compaq released the iPAQ Pocket PC. Whereas the focus of laptop computing was predominantly on portability and mobile access to documents and applications available on desktop computers, palmtop computing introduced an additional focus on applications and interaction styles designed specifically for mobile devices and mobile users.

The PDA generation of mobile devices represented a number of distinct interaction design choices and form factors. Most notably they introduced the combination of a relatively small touch-sensitive screen and a separate pen (or stylus) for user interaction. Using the stylus the user could interact with content directly on the screen and enter text via an on-screen keyboard or through handwriting recognition software. Other interaction design innovations included function buttons for accessing pre-defined applications and functions, navigation keys for operating menus, and the "one-click" dock for synchronizing with a stationary computer and for charging. While the Psion series 3–5 replicated a "laptop in miniature" design, the Newton, PalmPilot, and iPAQ all represented a fundamentally new mobile computing form factor where the majority of the device's surface was used for its display. In terms of interaction design, the PalmPilot, in particular, was a product of careful and detailed rethinking of the emerging class of handheld computers; what they should look and feel like, what functions they should perform, and how they should perform them. As an example, the creator of the PalmPilot, Jeff Hawkins, later explained how he carried blocks of wood with him in different sizes and shapes until he had reached the perfect physical form for the device (Bergman and Haitani 2000).

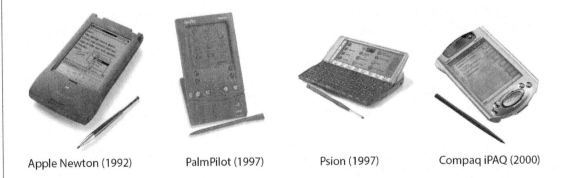

Apple Newton (1992)   PalmPilot (1997)   Psion (1997)   Compaq iPAQ (2000)

Figure 1.3: Mobile computers in the 1990–2000's.

With the emergence of PDAs came also new categories of applications developed specifically for mobile devices and users. The devices each had their own operating systems, optimized for their particular screen sizes and input capabilities, and a suite of standard applications for calendars, contacts, note taking, and email. Adding to this, a wide range of third-party applications soon became available for purchase, or, as something new, downloadable via the Internet. By the late 1990's application development specifically for mobile devices was an acknowledged research area and profession, and in 1998 the first international workshop on Human-Computer Interaction with Mobile Devices (Mobile HCI'98) was held in Glasgow specifically addressing the emerging challenge of interaction design and user experiences for mobile devices, systems and services.

1.3   CONNECTIVITY

The third wave of mobile computing had its origins in wireless telecommunication. As early as 1973 a Motorola team led by Martin Cooper developed and patented a handheld mobile phone concept that led to the first commercial mobile phone small enough to be carried, the DynaTAC 8000X, in 1983.

Figure 1.4: The first handheld cell phone: Motorola DynaTAC 8000X (1983).

In the 1980's and early 1990's mobile phones were not really considered to be computers. However, with the introduction of the digital GSM mobile phone system in 1991, which also included the Short Message Service (SMS) communication component, the complexity and functionality of handsets began evolving rapidly. So did the uptake of mobile phone technology by the broad population worldwide. This meant that mobile phone developers were suddenly faced with a huge challenge of interaction design not only for making phone calls, but also for handling contacts, calendars, text-based messages, and browsing the Internet. In the late 1990's, interaction design for mobile phones was unarguably dominated by the work at Nokia, which led to a series of groundbreaking handsets. The challenges of the time were to design for tiny low-resolution displays and for input capabilities limited to a 12-key numeric keypad along side a small number of function and navigation keys. One of the first mobile phones explicitly resulting from a careful process of interaction design in the 1990's was the Nokia 3110. It introduced a simple graphical menu system and the "Navi-key" concept for simplifying user interaction—an interaction design that reached the hands of more than 300 million users through subsequent Nokia handsets (Lindholm et al. 2003). In 1999, the basic interaction design of the Nokia 3110 was extended with T9 predictive text for SMS messaging, games, customisable ring tones, and changeable covers for the extremely successful Nokia 3210.

Nokia 3110 (1995)   Nokia 3210 (1999)   Nokia 7110 (1999)

Figure 1.5: Three mobile interaction design milestones: Navi-key, T9, and WAP.

In the late 1990's, the enormous, and completely unexpected, uptake of the Short Message Service (SMS) inspired attempts to bring the Internet to mobile handsets too. This led to the development of the Wireless Application Protocol (WAP) allowing simplified websites to be viewed on small displays and paving the way for Internet access on mobile devices. The first mobile phone to feature a WAP browser was the Nokia 7110. In response to the need for scrolling through long WAP pages it also featured the first "Navi-roller" thumb wheel. As an interesting example of interaction design, the 7110 also featured a *spring-loaded* cover concealing the keypad, which was inspired by the film The Matrix where the main character uses an earlier Nokia phone modified by the film's production crew to have this functionality. "Life imitating art" (Wilde 1889) you could say. WAP, however, never lived up to its expectations due to slow data transfer and poor usability (Ramsay and Nielsen 2000; Nielsen 2000) and was soon superseded by access to the real web on mobile devices. Nevertheless, mobile phone design in the 1990's had a fundamental and lasting impact on the future of mobile computing.

1.4   CONVERGENCE

One of the most interesting eras of mobile computing began when different types of specialized mobile devices began converging into new types of hybrid devices with fundamentally different form factors and interaction designs. The first phase of this was the emergence of "smart phones," which combined the functionality of a PDA with that of a mobile phone. The development of smart phones involved exploration of a wide range of form factors and interaction designs and led to a series of innovative solutions. Many of these involved designs where the physical shape of the device could be changed depending on what the user wanted to use it for. Other designs, like the Blackberry, introduced a "wide-body mobile phone" form factor with a PDA size display and a miniature QWERTY keyboard in place of the traditional 12-key numeric keypad. The first smart phone that as well as making phone calls could also be used for calendars, addresses, notes, e-mail, fax and games was the IBM Simon from 1992. It had no physical buttons but only a touch screen, which could be operated with a finger or a stylus.

IBM Simon (1992)   Nokia 9000 (1996)   Ericsson R380 (2000)   Blackberry 5810 (2002)

Figure1.6: Smartphones exploring different physical form factors and interaction styles.

The second phase of convergence combined mobile phones with various rich media capabilities, such as digital cameras, music players, video recording and playback, and television and radio reception. Whereas smart phones were attractive for business professional's work activities and productivity, multimedia phones were attractive for everyday people's leisure, fun and socialising.

Sharp J-SH04 (2001)   Nokia N-Gage (2003)   Nokia N90 (2005)   Sony Ericsson W600 (2005)

Figure 1.7: Converged mobile devices: camera-phones, game-phone and walkman-phone.

The most notable example of convergence for leisure was the invention of the camera phone. The first mobile phone to feature a digital camera was the Sharp J-SH04 from 2001. It was only available in Japan through the i-mode mobile Internet service, but the rest of the world soon followed. Two years later more camera phones were sold than digital cameras, and in 2006 half the world's mobile phones had a built-in camera—making Nokia the biggest brand of digital cameras and forcing prominent brands such as Minolta and Konica out of the camera business. By 2009 there were more than 1.9 billion camera phones in existence, and mobile phone photography had already had a huge social impact through new ways of capturing and sharing photographs over the Internet (cf. Kindberg et al. 2005; Gye 2007). Whereas early camera phones were clearly phones with cameras, novel interaction design led to several converged devices truly blurring the boundaries between the two (Murphy et al. 2005). As an example, it can be hard to tell if the Nokia N90 is a phone or a camcorder. Another converged functionality to become widely available on mobile phones was the ability to listen to digital music. Most notably Sony re-launched its successful "Walkman" brand of the 1980's in the shape of the converged Sony Ericsson W600 in 2005. With the W44 multimedia phone from 2006, they even went a step further and extended video and music playback with the ability to watch and listen to digital TV and radio. Convergence also led to the creation of hybrid game-phones like the Nokia N-Gage with form factors resembling handheld game consoles.

The fundamental driver behind the trend of convergence is that mobile user experience is proportionally related to the functional scope of interactive mobile devices and systems: "more means more" (Murphy et al. 2005). As a consequence, convergence has often been criticized for generating weak general solutions with usability comparable to the Swiss army knife: clumsy technology with a wide range of functions, none of which are ideal in isolation (see e.g., Norman 1998, Bergman 2000, Buxton 2001). However, in my view the real strength of convergence should not be sought in the simple availability of several functions implemented in the same device. Rather it should be found in the potential creation of something new and hybrid that facilitates use that wasn't possible before, like for example taking pictures and sharing them immediately with your friends, browsing the Internet on your phone, or purchasing music directly on your iPod.

1.5   DIVERGENCE

Contrasting the convergence approach, the trend of *divergence* suggested a single function/many devices or "information appliance" approach where each device is "designed to perform a specific activity, such as music, photography, or writing" (Bergman 2000). The driving force behind this line of thought is that having a wide range of good specialized tools is better than a general one that does not perform any task particularly well. Specialized tools facilitate optimisation of functionality over time and refinement of well-known paradigms of use. The fundamental view promoted by the trend of divergence is that mobile user experience is *inversely* proportionate to the functional scope of interactive mobile devices and systems: "less is more" (Murphy et al. 2005).

Apple iPod (2001)   Archos Gmini (2004)   Sony PSP (2004)   iPod Video (2005)

Figure 1.8: Specialized mobile media and gaming devices.

The 2000's saw the emergence a wide range of diverged mobile devices dedicated to do one specific task really well, particularly mobile music players, video players and games. Of course, functionally dedicated mobile devices were not a new phenomenon as, for example, early mobile devices such as pocket calculators, cell phones, GPS receivers, digital cameras, and PDAs could unarguably be classified as information appliances too. But what was interesting about the trend of divergence in the early 2000's was that it was a deliberate interaction design choice and not a technological necessity. Probably the most legendary example of an information appliance was the Apple iPod from 2001. Although not the first mobile digital music player, its interaction design, including the integration with iTunes and later the iTunes Music Store, fundamentally changed global music consumption and purchasing behaviour. Although most mobile phones on the market in the mid 2000's were able to play MP3 files, people still preferred to carry an additional device, the iPod, for playing their music as it provided a better user experience for that particular task, and the device itself had become a popular fashion item. In late 2010 the total number of iPods sold had exceeded 290 million units. Other diverged mobile devices included video players like the Archos

Gmini from 2004, the Sony PSP game and video console, and later versions of the iPod extended with video playback capability but within the same basic information appliance interaction design.

The interaction design challenge of a diverged mobile device is considerably different from that of a converged one because its functional scope is much narrower. However, as diverged devices are by definition typically used in concert with a plethora of other interactive devices and systems unknown to the designer, there is a huge interaction design challenge in supporting good and flexible integration and "convergence-in-use" (Murphy et al. 2005).

1.6   APPS

In June 2007 Apple launched the iPhone. Like many of its contemporaries this was a converged mobile device functioning as a camera phone, portable media player, and Internet client with e-mail, web browsing, and high-speed wireless network connectivity. However, rather than being just another incremental step in the evolution of converged mobile devices, the iPhone represented a significant rethinking of the design of mobile interactions and a series of notable interaction design choices. It featured a large high-resolution capacitive multi-touch display with simple gesture capabilities such as swiping and pinching, and departed completely from the predominant use of physical keys and a stylus for text entry and interaction. Instead of navigating large and deep hierarchies of menus, the user experience was much more fluid and aesthetic, and the phone was both extremely easy and pleasurable to use. The iPhone also featured a number of embedded context sensors, which changed the orientation mode of the display depending on how it was held, as originally proposed in a UIST conference paper by Hinckley et al. (2000), and changed the mode of the phone application when held close to the face during a call. The later inclusion of GPS and a digital compass extended this "context-awareness" capability to also enable location-based services.

On the software side, the iPhone's web browser actually made it possible to access web content on a mobile device with a positive user experience, and many soon described handling email on the iPhone as favourable compared to its desktop counterparts. Dedicated applications provided direct access to watching video content from YouTube and purchasing music from the iTunes Store. In concert, this meant that people actually started using their mobile device as a *preferred* gateway to the Internet, rather than as a last resort. Consequently, iPhone OS dominated the total amount of mobile web traffic worldwide by mid 2009 (Admob 2009). In addition to this, data and media content can be integrated seamlessly with the user's other devices and computers at home or at work through cloud computing services such as MobileMe in a way never seen before in mobile interaction design, illustrating initial steps toward the creation of *digital ecosystems* of mobile and stationary computer systems connected through the Internet.

The iPhone completely redefined mobile computing and set new standards for mobile interaction design and user experiences that other companies, such as Google and HTC, still struggled to match up to four years later with the Android open source mobile operating system and associated online application store. In many ways, the iPhone was the device that mobile interaction design researchers had envisioned for a decade, and its enormous uptake worldwide, with over 120 million iOS enabled devices sold by September 2010, confirms that we were indeed right in our speculations about what people would want to do with mobiles—if only we could provide them with a good enough interaction design and user experience. The biggest impact of the iPhone, however, was not only in the interaction design of the device itself and in the high quality of its native applications. As it turned out, it was in the creation of an interaction design that provided users with easy access to a vast and unprecedented amount of *applications* for their mobile device.

In 2008 Apple launched the online "App Store" which provided a mechanism by which iPhone users could easily download, and pay for, third-party application content directly from their mobile device. These Apps span a range of functionalities, including social networking, productivity tools, personal utilities, games, navigation, and advertising for movies and TV shows. For creating this application content, an iPhone OS software development kit (SDK) was released for free along with a business model where Apple handles payments and distribution while leaving App creators with 70% of the profit. By 2012 more than 25 billion Apps had been downloaded from a selection of more than 500,000, making this hugely profitable for both Apple and for the individual third-party creators of particularly popular Apps, which, in return, has motivated the creation of even more application content. As an indication of the incredible size of this business, third party mobile software developers generated a total income of $2 billion by selling their products through the Apple App store in less than three years. Contrary to developing mobile applications in Java 2 Platform, Micro Edition (J2ME) or Qualcomm's Binary Runtime Environment for Wireless (BREW), developing in iPhone SDK involves no need for customizing applications for a vast range of different handsets, which means that more time can be spent on application design. Also, in sharp contrast to the generally horrific mobile phone user interfaces for installing especially J2ME software, the iPhone provides not only a supply chain and billing model out-of-the-box but also an application shopping user experience that is *positive in itself*. Hence, prior to the iPhone, downloading and installing software onto a mobile phone or PDA was something only technology-savvy people would do. Today this is common practice for millions of users of all ages and computing experience.

As an interesting effect of the iPhone-approach to mobile interaction design, improving the hardware specification of devices was suddenly surpassed in importance in favour of improving the software that is available for them. This is evidenced in the pace and scope of software developments and updates compared to equivalent hardware ones. This is an important shift within the design of mobile interactions, and indicates that a level of stability has been reached in terms of physical form factors and basic input and output capabilities, in favour of a focus on *applications and content*.

Figure 1.9: The Apple iPhone and iPad (2007 and 2010).

Apple's success of the iPhone lead to a third endeavour within mobile computing, the iPad, which was released in April 2010. Initial media reaction was mixed, but commercial uptake was unprecedented, and the iPad was sold in over 2 million units in its first two months, reaching 15 million units sold by the end of the year. While Microsoft's explicit interaction design approach for PDAs and tablets had long been to replicate the Windows 95 OS (Zuberec 2000), Apple took the opposite approach with the iPad tablet and based it on iPhone OS rather than MacOSX. This was a surprising move for many, admittedly including myself, but had the effect of reinterpreting, and subsequently redefining, the so-far troubled category of "tablet computers" into a new category of *mobile devices* that are not just laptops without keyboards. Although criticized for being a closed system, the strength of the iPad lay in the user experience created through its meticulous interaction design, which invited the already growing community of iPhone interaction designers and application developers to explore the tablet form factor. Until then, nobody had cared to create web or native application content for tablets (Chen 2010), but with the iPad, tablets suddenly became one of the most interesting and promising mobile platforms on Earth, and by March 2011 there were more than 65,000 applications available for the iPad.

1.7   DIGITAL ECOSYSTEMS

As we have moved into the second decade of the new millennium the challenges facing mobile computing and interaction design continue to evolve. The technical capabilities of our mobile devices have improved significantly to the point where factors such as screen real estate, input capabilities, processing power, network speed, and battery lifetime are much less of an issue than only half a decade ago. At the same time, we have also become sufficiently skilled at designing for relatively small screens and for the different input capabilities of mobile devices that millions of ordinary people are actually able to download and use the applications being developed, and are even willing to pay for some of them. To a large extent, therefore, we have now successfully solved the majority of problems facing mobile interaction researchers and designers in the past. However, as the history of all areas of computing have shown us, it is highly unlikely that we have reached an end point. As in the past, the technology and interaction design we are witnessing today is just the starting point for the continuing evolution of the technology and interaction design of tomorrow. But what are then the challenges and opportunities for the design of mobile interactions to come? What will the next wave of mobile computing be about?

Fueled by the enormous interest and uptake of "post-PC devices" like smart phones and tablets by the general population, it is not unreasonable to speculate that a major platform shift away from desktop computing is imminent. Mobile devices are becoming more and more important and widespread. They will soon be the dominating point of access to the Internet, and in combination with the growth of cloud computing they will soon dominate peoples' use of computational power. Importantly, what we are witnessing here is not just the development of even smarter smart phones with improved abilities to imitate desktop PCs in miniature. It is a radical evolution of a major computing platform for new applications allowing us to do things that couldn't be done before. This may well be a genuine paradigm shift for mobile computing and mobile interaction design.

In my belief, the next wave of mobile computing and interaction design is going to be about the creation of *digital ecosystems* (Miller et al. 2010, Sørensen et al. 2014) in which mobile computing plays a central role in concert with other ubiquitous computing resources. This challenges us to move beyond considering interactive mobile devices, systems and services as entities that can meaningfully be designed and studied in isolation from the larger use context or artifact ecologies (Jung et al. 2008, Bødker and Klokmose 2011) that they are a part of. Yes, mobile computers, in various forms, play hugely important roles in most peoples' everyday lives, but they are not the only technologies and artifacts we make use of at home or at work, or in the space between. Most people use multiple mobile devices for different purposes, but they also use a multitude of stationary or embedded computer systems, at work, at home, in our cars, or in the city around us. In concert this makes up a rich digital ecosystem of interactive devices, systems, and services often referred to as ubiquitous or pervasive computing, in which mobile computing is a central, but not the only, component. The challenge of designing mobile interactions in such ubiquitous and pervasive information societies is to facilitate the creation of interactive devices, systems, and services that fit well into this ecosystem of other devices, systems, and services, as well as into the rich new use patterns, for work and leisure, created by these technologies and their users. Like any other type of ecosystem, understanding, creating, and maintaining digital ecosystems requires a holistic perspective on the totality and ecology of the system at play, and not just detailed views on each of its individual components. As argued earlier, it is my position that this cannot be achieved well through a technology- or a user-centered approach, but requires a change of the unit of analysis toward one that continually includes both these viewpoints.

The digital ecology wave of mobile computing will build on the achievements of previous eras within hardware miniaturization, connectivity, new form factors, input devices, interaction styles, applications, convergence, divergence, and content, but it will broaden the scope to include the wider context of use and an explicit sensitivity for the contextual factors that influence the user experience. It is going to be about creating interactive devices, systems, and services that respond to the broad and diverse aspects of human life, and that not only provide utility and are easy to use, but also provide pleasure and fit naturally into peoples' complex and dynamic lives of constantly changing settings and situations. My position here is that this will best be achieved through careful attention to the details, richness, and dynamics of *form-context ensembles* during all phases of mobile interaction design and system development: from initial domain studies and analysis through creative design, implementation of actual interactive systems, evaluation studies, and analysis of their outcomes.

CHAPTER 2

Interaction Design

I will now turn my attention toward the notion of interaction design. The term interaction design was coined by Bill Moggridge and Bill Verplank in the late 1980's, and is about "designing interactive products to support the way people communicate and interact in their everyday and working lives" (Sharp et al. 2007 p. 8), or more broadly about "the design of everything that is both digital and interactive" (Moggridge 2007 p. 660) with particular attention to its subjective and qualitative aspects. In other words, it is about creating life and work enhancing user experiences through the design, development, construction, and implementation of interactive products, devices, systems, and services.

Today, interactive products are typically computer-based, and this means that interaction design is relevant within all disciplines, fields, and approaches that concern themselves with research and design of computer-based systems for people. Hence, alongside design practices such as graphic and industrial design, academic disciplines such as psychology and sociology, and multi/interdisciplinary fields such as human-computer interaction and information systems, interaction design also involves the technical academic disciplines of computer science and engineering. However, interaction design differs from each of these practices, disciplines, and fields by having a different, overall, focus and purpose. It is concerned with the *totality* of the user experience of interactive products and with all of the factors that may contribute to their successful creation. When we design computer-based interactive systems, we are not just designing how it appears but also how it behaves. We are designing how people and technology interact (Moggridge 2007). As described by Winograd (1997), doing interaction design can in many ways be compared to doing architecture. The architect is concerned with people and their interactions within the building being created. For example, does the space fit the lives or work styles of the family or business that is going to inhabit it? Does the flow within and between rooms work well? Are functionally related spaces in close proximity? And so on. Supporting the work of the architect, engineers are concerned with the structural soundness and construction methods of the building, and knowledge from other disciplines, such as human factors and social sciences may also influence the architect's ability to create functional and liveable spaces. Just like a good architect understands these other relevant disciplines, so does a good interaction designer. However, just like there is a difference between designing and building a house there is also a difference between designing an interactive product and engineering its software (Sharp et al. 2007 p. 9).

This analogy also illustrates how interaction design differs from the fields of human-computer interaction and human factors. Whereas HCI and HF have traditionally focused on the relatively narrow study of human-machine interaction and the major factors surrounding this in order to optimize user interfaces and overall system performance, interaction design is "about shaping our everyday life through digital artifacts—or work, for play, and for entertainment" (Smith 2007 p. xi). In this way, interaction design "has cast its net much wider, being concerned with the theory, research, and practice of designing user experiences for all manner of technologies, systems and products" (Sharp et al. 2007 p. 10). The goal, and the challenge, of interaction design is to make powerful computing technology fit into the peoples' work and private lives rather than forcing peoples' lives to fit technology. In order to achieve this goal, solutions produced by interaction designers must be appropriate to their context (Smith 2007).

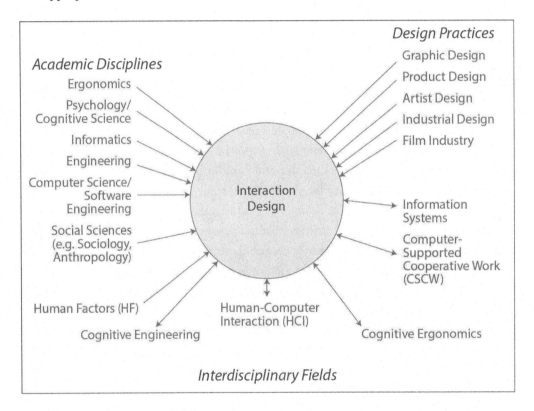

Figure 2.1: Academic disciplines, design practices, and research fields concerned with Interaction Design (from Sharp et al. 2007 p. 10).

There is a difference between interaction design *practice* and interaction design *research*. Interaction design practice is about creating concrete interactive systems and solutions to a particular design problem by applying the knowledge and approaches of the discipline. Interaction design research is about creating and improving this knowledge and these approaches, which is often done through studies of interaction design practice. Hence, it can be argued that interaction design is merely a practice and that it is based on the cumulative sum of research in all of its contributing disciplines and research fields, such as human-computer interaction, industrial design, psychology, sociology, computer science, etc., as depicted in Figure 2.1 (Sharp et al. 2007 p. 10). The risk of such a view, however, is that it presents interaction design as a research-less discipline and distributes interaction design research on a large number of individual disciplines relevant for, but external to, interaction design itself. Thinking about disciplinary borders, which I will return to later, this view essentially keeps interaction design within the confinements of multidisciplinarity without enabling the potentials of cross-disciplinary collaboration in the creation of new types of knowledge and methodological approaches. The opposite view, which I share and promote in this book, is that interaction design is, or rather *should be*, a discipline not only with its own practice, but also with its own research agenda and challenges, and that interaction design practice and research are both inherently interdisciplinary.

There is also a difference between being an interaction designer and being an interaction design researcher. Not all interaction designers are skilled researchers, and not all interaction design researchers work as interaction designers. However, given the fundamentally creative and design-oriented nature of the discipline of interaction design, it is my fundamental and strong belief that being a good interaction design researcher requires skills and talents as an interaction designer too.

2.1   MOBILE INTERACTION DESIGN

Mobile interaction design is an area of interaction design that is concerned specifically with the creation of user experiences with interactive products, devices, systems, and services that are not stationary but that people can take with them. It is enabled by advances in mobile computing—as described earlier—that have allowed designers and system developers to conceive interactive products that are small enough to be carried with us, held in our hands, or even worn, while also providing computational power and network capabilities sufficient enough for enabling useful and attractive interactive systems and services. This includes handheld and wearable devices, PDAs, mobile phones, smart phones, portable digital media players, handheld games, etc., as well as the software applications and services that run on these devices or can be accessed from them. However, mobile interaction design is not only facilitated and driven by advances in computer science and engineering. It is also increasingly advanced by our ability to develop new use practices for mobile computing and to include and appropriate available and emerging mobile computer and network technologies into new and innovative interactive products and solutions. Hence, we have long gone beyond the "anytime anywhere" mobile computing hype of the late 1990's and grown much more sensible aspirations to develop "mobiles that work at the right time, and that know their place—that fit in" (Jones and Marsden 2006).

The challenges of mobile interaction design have changed and evolved over time as new technologies were developed and new use practices emerged. Early mobile interaction design dealt with the physical design of portable computers. This evolved into a focus on input devices and interaction styles suitable for handheld operation and mobile use. For mobile phones the interaction design challenge has primarily been a matter of reducing physical size while optimizing the use of limited display real estate and the standard 12-key numeric keypad for more and more possible applications. With the emergence of functionally hybrid and more complex devices, the interaction design challenge became about developing new forms and shapes of devices as well as developing new types of applications available on them, without making the devices (even) harder to use. For the growing range of functionally dedicated mobile devices like digital cameras and media players the interaction design challenge became about facilitating peoples' "orchestration" of all these devices, and their content, in increasingly complex ecosystems of interactive computer systems and digital data.

Today, the challenge of designing mobile interactions is very much about the development of *software applications*. The physical device form factor appears to have stabilized, for some time at least, on the basic size, shape and interaction capability introduced by the Apple iPhone in 2007, which has remained unchanged for more than four years and been replicated by all major handset producers. This has shifted focus toward downloadable and purchasable third-party application content available for these devices, in the form of relatively small "Apps" with highly specialized functionality, designed not only by large software corporations but also by small companies and even individuals, including students. By late 2010 more than 300,000 third-party applications were available from the Apple App Store and more than 80,000 were available from Google's Android Market. In less than 3 years more than 10 billion Apps were downloaded for the iPhone and iPod Touch. However, although a lot of interesting and innovative new mobile applications are appearing in Google's and Apple's online stores every day, and application developers and interaction designers world wide are pushing the boundaries of what mobile computer devices are being used for, the state of current mobile application design can be compared to the state of the web in the mid to late 1990's. There is a lot of excitement and interest, the development tools are easily accessible, and there is a huge audience of potential users. Exceeding the potentials of the web in the mid 1990's there are even well-established digital supply chains and mechanisms for micro-payments. But as with the web 15 years ago, we haven't yet seen or understood the significance and scope of the impact that third-party application design for mobile devices will have on all aspects of our lives, for work as well as for leisure.

2.2   RESEARCH IMPACT ON PRACTICE

Much of the future impact of mobile computing envisioned above will be driven by skillful and creative design of mobile interactions conceived by entrepreneurial developers and designers who understand how to create useful and enjoyable utility and user experience that fits the users needs, desires, and contexts of use. Unfortunately, however, the current research-based literature on mobile interaction design does not provide as much foundation as we probably could for these developers and designers to base their innovations and interaction design on, nor much methodological guidance on how to approach the process. Whereas there are a lot of research-based books about user interface and interaction design for desktop applications and websites there is not yet a lot of equivalent literature available about mobile interaction design. Although mobile computing has a history of approximately three decades, and interaction design has played an important role throughout about 2/3 of this history, only one good general textbook, by Matt Jones and Gary Marsden (2006), has been published on the topic to date. And although this book is indeed a brilliant starting point for addressing the particular challenges of *mobile* interaction design, it still doesn't have the completeness and depth of equivalent human-computer interaction and interaction design primers such as Laurel (1990), Shneiderman (1998), Preece et al. (1994), Winograd (1996), Raskin (2000), Dix et al. (2004), Benyon et al. (2005), Lauesen (2005), Bagnara and Smith (2006), Preece et al. (2002), and Rogers et al. (2011). This is potentially an opportunity missed for large-scale real-world impact on mobile interaction design *practice* in respect to the massive amount of good interaction design research that has been done within the field over the last decade and a half. While it might indicate that the area of mobile interaction design still hasn't stabilized enough for general guidelines, principles, methods, and techniques to evolve, it also demonstrates an opportunity, and a need, to push forward on developing such foundational work further.

Several of the textbooks that *do* exist on aspects of interaction design for mobile devices, systems and services, such as Helal et al. (1999), Weiss (2002) Ballard (2007), Fling (2009), and Frederick and Lal (2010), essentially target application development for particular and very specific classes of devices and software platforms, and address ephemeral technical limitations such as particular operating systems, low screen resolution, reduced processing power, limited memory, and poor bandwidth. While unarguably useful when designing for these exact platforms, the weakness of such types of works is that they are almost too practical. They are highly vulnerable to technological advances and therefore quickly rendered irrelevant as new devices and platforms emerge. As a consequence, they usually end up as short-lived and overly specific user interface guidelines tied to a specific point in time, and not as generally applicable and timeless principles for interaction design. Distilling the essence of these works—the higher-level challenges and solutions that apply beyond specific devices and platforms—would be useful for moving the field of mobile interaction design forward. But such work has not yet been done systematically and in depth.

As a step in the right direction though, a different class of textbooks on mobile interaction design is the collection of case study-like accounts for successful and influential design solutions, such as Eric Bergman's *Information Appliances and Beyond* (2000), Lindholm et al.'s *Mobile Usability: how Nokia changed the face of the mobile phone* (2003), parts of Bill Moggridge's *Designing Inter-*

actions (2007), and Bondo et al.'s *iPhone User Interface Design Projects*"(2009). These writings aim to capture universally important lessons learned from the experience of actual mobile interaction designers. They provide interaction design as well as methodological insight about influential solutions and how they came about. The potential weakness of *these* works, however, is that they easily end up being anecdotal and difficult to transfer into present time's design challenges. To support such transfer and transcendence of knowledge, we must provide not only the case study accounts, but also analysis across these case studies that elevates our learning from the concrete and specific level to the abstract and general. This accumulation of an abstract and general body of knowledge is probably better suited for a design researcher than for a design practitioner, and it is what the work presented in this book aspires to contribute to.

2.3   MULTI- AND INTERDISCIPLINARITY

Interaction design, whether it is mobile or not mobile, is a field of research that involves several disciplines and works across disciplinary boundaries (Sharp et al. 2007, p. 10). It is widely accepted that research across disciplines is difficult, and consequently, in practice, a lot of such research "actually works at the level of being *multidisciplinary* (or pluridisciplinary): where a group of researchers from different disciplines cooperate by working together on the same problem toward a common goal, but continue to do so using theories, tools, and methods from their own discipline and occasionally using the output from each other's work" (Rogers et al. 2005). Today, mobile interaction design is an example of such a *multidisciplinary* area. This means that it involves a mixture of disciplines, such as computer science, engineering, human factors, psychology, sociology, design, etc., and that these disciplines each contribute to a composite body of knowledge about the design of mobile interactions. Being multidisciplinary means that the challenges of mobile interaction design are approached from different perspectives and with different competences, and that research is therefore diversified and broad. This ensures outcomes that span widely, from new technological endeavours to exploration of new use domains. However, the problem of being multidisciplinary is, by definition, that each discipline retains its own identity, methodologies, assumptions and aims, and that these are not changed or influenced by the other disciplines within the multidisciplinary relationship. Although multidisciplinary research involves several disciplines "each discipline makes a separate contribution" (Moore and Lottridge 2010). This non-integrative mixture of disciplines basically means that there is a shared interest in the topic of mobile computing from within multiple disciplines, but that each of these disciplines treats the common topic of interest in their own way and with their own focus, as defined and guided by their individual school of thought.

The idea of mobile interaction design has appeared in different disciplines at around the same time, but cooperation between these multiple disciplines is largely "mutual and cumulative but not interactive" (Augsburg 2005, p. 56). This underlying separation between disciplines can be seen in the general observation that although the field is concerned with the same overall topic of *interac-*

tion between people and technology, most specific research is in fact focused primarily on one or the other. It is either technology- or user-centered, and as pointed out by Rasmussen (2007) when making such clear-cut distinction between technology- or user-centered approaches, a valuable dialectic between the two tends to disappear at the cost of possible synthesis of the two opposing interests and forces at a higher level (Nonaka and Toyama 2002, Dahlbom and Mathiassen 1993). As we observed in an empirical study comparing these two disciplinarily different approaches to the development of two similar interactive mobile systems (Kjeldskov and Howard 2004; Jones and Marsden 2006, pp. 88-89) applying either view in isolation has a notable negative impact on the quality and completeness of the produced outcomes, and producing well-functioning and usable mobile interaction design would be supported better by explicitly combining and integrating technology- and user-centered approaches.

In contrast to *multidisciplinarity*, *interdisciplinarity* crosses the traditional boundaries between disciplines or schools of thought as new challenges, needs, and professions emerge, and blends the involved disciplines including their identities, methodologies, assumptions and aims. It *connects* and *integrates* several academic schools of thought or professions in the pursuit of a common task, along with their specific standpoints, and is not just different disciplines pasted together but rather an "integration and synthesis of ideas and methods" (Moore and Lottridge 2010). On the basis of this, interdisciplinary research derives "novel concepts, methods and theoretical frameworks through the melding of concepts, methods and theoretical frameworks coming from different disciplines" (Rogers et al. 2005). Interdisciplinary research areas often emerge from mutual beliefs that traditional disciplines are insufficient for addressing an important topic on their own, or in a simple non-integrative mixture with each other, due to the topic's multi-faceted, or even transdisciplinary, nature where a unity of knowledge is needed across disciplines, or even beyond them. Where multidisciplinarity approaches a problem space using a *coordinated* effort from *distinct* methodological foundations, interdisciplinarity approaches a problem space using an *integrated* effort from *combined* methodological foundations (Blevis and Stolterman 2009). Hence, the main difference between multi- and interdisciplinarity lies in the way research is conducted, and as a consequence of this also in the types of outcomes produced.

The position that I put forward here is that in order to better inform the creation of interactive mobile devices, systems, and services in the future, mobile interaction design needs to evolve from being a multidisciplinary research field to becoming an interdisciplinary one. This position echoes the message from Steve Jobs since early 2010 that the key to Apple's position in the "post-PC era" of interactive mobile systems and devices such as the iPhone and iPad is credited to the explicit belief at Apple that technology alone is not enough, but that "it's technology married with liberal arts, married with the humanities, that yields us the result that makes our hearts sing" (Jobs 2011). According to Jobs, this explicit interdisciplinarity sits "at the intersection between technology and liberal arts," where technical sciences facilitate the creation of "extremely advanced products from a technology point of view" (Jobs 2010) and contemporary liberal art disciplines, such as literature, philosophy, history, science, and design facilitate making them "intuitive, easy to use, fun to use, so that they really fit the users—the users don't have to come to them, they come to the user." This interdisciplinarity is what drives Apple's ability to develop new mobile interaction design that repeatedly pushes the boundary of what is technically possible and, at the same time, is almost immediately embraced globally and soon taken for granted by millions of people.

As pointed out by Rogers et al. (2005), it is not problematic to use the terms multi- and inter-disciplinarity interchangeably if simply referring to collaboration between people from different disciplines working on a common problem. However, depending on the underlying rationale for the collaborative activity, the two can have rather different meanings. Put simply, "bringing together a group of experts from different disciplines or professions to contribute to a single project, which would not be able to be accomplished by any one profession alone" is different from when "a group of researchers from distinct disciplines try to generate novel concepts and integrate different levels of explanation" (Rogers et al. 2005). Here, the former denotes multidisciplinarity where each researcher contributes to the project with unique expertise, whereas the latter denotes interdisciplinarity where new research questions are dealt with. Achieving interdisciplinarity can be very difficult. Whereas multidisciplinarity can be done through coordination of research efforts, there are many more obstacles to the "cross-fertilization" of ideas required in interdisciplinarity, including incommensurability of concepts, dissimilar units of analysis, variation in world view, etc. (Rogers et al. 2005). This raises the fundamental question of when interdisciplinarity is needed and, and how it then can be achieved in practice.

Basically, interdisciplinarity is desirable when reaching a point where the constraints of ones own discipline prevents any further significant progress, and researchers are forced to work in the outer periphery of their field and, in doing so, are having to forge new ones (The Royal Society 1996). According to Rogers et al. (2005) there are two types of impetus leading to such circumstances motivating input from several disciplines: cases where "an existing problem has simply become too large for a single discipline to cope with," and cases where "something external to the disciplines has forced itself on their attention." Good examples of these two types of cases are the attempt to develop a comprehensive cognitive science program, which held interdisciplinarity as an ideal, and the evolution of the fields of HCI and CSCW, where applied interdisciplinarity was motivated by technological advances within computing. However, for both two cases the project of forging interdisciplinarity faced significant challenges, and it can be questioned how successful the endeavors were. For cognitive science, a major limitation was that the key issues of the "interdiscipline" could still meaningfully, and sometimes advantageously, be studied within a single existing discipline, i.e., x (Norman 1990). For HCI and CSCW a major limitation has been to break away from the multidisciplinary mindset of simply dividing up the joint challenge into coordinated applied disciplinarity, and to really tie together and make mappings across concepts from different disciplines toward the development of unified theory (Bannon 1992). Hence, according to Rogers et al. (2005) "the jury is still out as to whether either HCI or CSCW have in fact been able to achieve any significant level of interdisciplinarity."

2.4   MODIFYING THE UNIT OF ANALYSIS

Mobile interaction design shares properties with both cases above. As with HCI and CSCW applied interdisciplinarity is motivated by technological advances, and as with cognitive science the ideal of interdisciplinarity is motivated by the fact that the full scope of the field is impossible to grasp from one perspective alone. But how can we then avoid repeating the modest success of interdisciplinarity within these related fields? According to Rogers et al. (2005) a possible key to achieving interdisciplinarity lies in explicitly transcending beyond current disciplinary dogma and units of analysis. "If true interdisciplinarity is ever to take off, then what is needed is a paradigm shift whereby a whole set of new issues and research questions are framed that force new ways of conceptualizing and working" (Rogers et al. 2005). This facilitates what they call "reconceptualizing the domain of interest through using a modified unit of analysis" whereby the scope can be broadened while still allowing the use of existing concepts and theory. As an example, the distributed cognition approach (Hutchins 1995) extended established cognitive science's focus on properties and processes inside a single person's mind to a system of cognitive systems involving several actors and their environment studied through "cognitive ethnography." Although such broadening of scope and change in level of abstraction is difficult and precarious, the benefit is that it has the potential to reveal phenomena that go across, and cannot be reduced to, existing units of analysis.

In relation to Bannon's (1992) concern that the goal of developing interdisciplinary unified theory within HCI and CSCW is fundamentally flawed due to the inherent incommensurability of theory, concepts, traditions, perspectives, etc., the significance of the more modest approach of changing the unit of analysis is that theoretical developments from such endeavours can advance our understanding of the field of interest through extending, adapting, and integrating *existing concepts and theories*. This can be seen as advantageous over creating completely new concepts and theories, which entail a risk of unintentionally disregarding legacy of previous accomplishments and achievements within the individual contributing disciplines, and potentially separating from valuable epistemological and methodological inheritance.

Classifying research as either multi- or interdisciplinary can sometimes be overly simplistic, as in reality there is a continuum between the two, "from multidisciplinary work with sharp boundaries between the disciplines at one end to the holistic approach of interdisciplinarity at the other" (The Royal Society 1996). This also means that going straight to complete holistic interdisciplinarity is usually not possible but requires evolution through several stages of involved disciplines becoming increasingly integrated as the shared problem is explored, developed, and defined. Redefining the unit of analysis can be seen as a way of stimulating such stepwise evolution toward interdisciplinarity by taking its offset in the knowledge and methodologies of existing disciplines, and aiming at developing better understanding of broader phenomena that are, in essence, new to all of those disciplines, and therefore also suitably peripheral to established belief systems.

In order to support the research field of mobile interaction design evolving from being a multidisciplinary area of research to becoming an interdisciplinary one, a change in the basic unit of analysis toward one with a wider scope that transcends the individual contributing disciplines' focus on either users or technologies may be called for. Similarly to Hutchins' (1995) broadening of scope toward "cognition in the wild," a good candidate for such modified unit of analysis, I argue, is the broader and more holistic phenomena of form-context convergence. Supporting this position, I am going to briefly turn my attention toward the role of context in the design of mobile interactions.

2.5   THE ROLE OF CONTEXT

Since the early days of mobile computing and mobile human-computer interaction, the use contexts of interactive mobile systems and devices have often been highlighted as being particularly important for system developers to "be aware of" and "take into account" when designing and building interactive mobile systems, and when evaluating and studying their use (cf. Johnson 1998, Rodden et al. 1998, Brown et al. 2000). Mobile use contexts have been described as being particularly challenging compared to, for example, the use contexts of traditional stationary office systems due to their highly dynamic, complex, and indeed mobile, nature. It has also often been suggested that when using an interactive mobile computer system other activities in the surrounding context are often more important than the actual interaction with and use of the system itself—walking down the street, socializing in a bar or café, or attending to a patient in a hospital.

There are many different definitions of context, and the debate on what constitutes context for mobile computing, and what role it plays, is ongoing. Early works within mobile computing referred to context as primarily the location of people and objects (Schilit and Theimer 1994). In more recent works, context has been extended to include a broader collection of factors such as physical and social aspects of an environment (McCullough 2004, Dourish 2004, Bradley and Dunlop 2002, Agre 2001, Dey 2001, Abowd and Mynatt 2000, Schmidt et al. 1999a, Crabtree and Rhodes 1998). Dey (2001) characterizes context as "any information that can be used to characterize the situation of an entity. An entity is a person, place, or object that is considered relevant to the interaction between a user and an application, including the user and the application themselves." Although this definition is quite complete, it is not very specific about what type of information could in fact be used to characterize such a situation. In contrast to this, Schmidt et al. (1999a) present a model of context with two distinct categories: human factors and physical environment. Human factors consist of the three categories: information about the user (profile, emotional state, etc), the user's social environment (presence of other people, group dynamics, etc), and the user's tasks (current activity, goals, etc.). Physical environment consist of the three categories: location (absolute and relative position, etc.), infrastructure (computational resources, etc.), and physical conditions (noise, light, etc.). This model provides a good catalog of specific contextual factors to complement broader definitions like the one by Dey (2001). Other works are not as comprehensive in their coverage of different contextual factors but go into detail about one or a few. In the works of Agre (2001) and McCullough (2004), particular importance is given to physical context consisting of architectural structures and elements of the built environment, for example, landmarks and pathways. In the works of Dourish (2001b, 2004), particular importance is given to social context including interaction with, and the behaviour of, people in an environment. Dourish (2004) also states that context cannot be defined as a stable description of a setting, but instead arises from, and is sustained by, the activities of people. Hence, it is continually being renegotiated and redefined in the course of action. These works provide us with additional contextual factors of particular relevance to mobile computing in context, and with the knowledge that what defines context is in itself contextually dependent.

The purpose here is not to challenge these existing definitions of context proposed in the literature. Instead, I subscribe to the definition by Dey (2001) and to the fact that several dimensions of context exist, and that the relevance of each of these for a particular interactive system or use situation is itself dependent on the specific situation. What is important here is the role that "context" can potentially play as a suitable central and mediating concept, or boundary object (Star and Griesemer 1989), in a holistic and interdisciplinary approach to designing mobile interactions. The context of mobile computing is something that several individual disciplines within mobile interaction design are concerned with, and that has influenced the shaping of methodology, technology and theory within and across the field's internal disciplinary boundaries. These different disciplines have each approached the challenge of contexts differently, and have yielded different types of responses.

In domain studies of mobile computing, where context plays an obvious central role as essentially the phenomenon under scrutiny, the challenge has been partly to understand theoretically what use contexts are and how they can be described, and partly to study empirically what characterizes specific use contexts of interest, and how the phenomenon of context can be studied and analyzed in ways that generate such understanding (e.g., Luff and Heath 1998, Dourish 2001b, Dourish 2004, Dey 2001, Ling 2001, Perry et al. 2001, Fortunati 2001, Green et al. 2001, Agre 2001, McCullough 2004, Chalmers 2004, Paay and Kjeldskov 2005, Paay and Kjeldskov 2008a, Aoki et al. 2009, Kostakos et al. 2009).

In systems development and design for mobile computing the challenge of context has primarily been about creating an appropriate fit between systems and context and how this can be supported structurally through new, or modified, systems development and design methods (e.g., Sharples et al. 2002, Mikkonen et al. 2002, Hosbond 2005, Paay 2008, de Sá and Carrico 2009, Paay et al. 2009a, Kjeldskov and Stage 2012).

In usability evaluation for mobile computing the challenge of context has primarily been to understand its role in relation to the scope, richness and validity of empirical findings and how usability tests can be carried out in contextually realistic settings through use of new or modified methods and techniques (e.g., Brewster 2002, Kjeldskov and Stage 2004, Kjeldskov et al. 2004, Kjeldskov et al. 2005, Betiol et al. 2005, Hagen et al. 2005, Kaikkonen et al. 2005, Rogers et al. 2007, Reichl et al. 2007, Oulasvirta 2009, Oulasvirta and Nyyssonen 2009, de Sá and Carrico 2009, Kjeldskov and Skov 2014).

In implementation of mobile computing the challenge of context has largely been about capturing, formalizing, and modelling this attribute in computational data models, how to make sense from such models, and how to use them in the construction of *context-aware* mobile systems that are responsive to their surroundings (e.g., Schilit and Theimer 1994, Crabtree and Rhodes 1998, Schmidt et al. 1999a, 1999b, Cheverst et al. 2000, Dix et al. 2000, Chen and Kotz 2000, Hinckley and Horvitz 2001, Dey 2001, Jameson 2001, Jones et al. 2004, Edwards 2005, Hinckley et al. 2005, Kjeldskov and Paay 2005, Kjeldskov and Skov 2007, Kjeldskov et al. 2010, Kjeldskov et al. 2013).

In user experience research for mobile computing the challenge of context has been to understand what impact rich and dynamic user contexts have on peoples' experience of using technology, and to describe how this user experience can be improved (e.g., Abowd and Mynatt 2000, Cheverst et al. 2001, Palen et al. 2000, Weilenmann 2001, Bradley and Dunlop 2002, Brown and Randell 2004, Paay and Kjeldskov 2008b, Bardram 2009, Little and Briggs 2009, Benford et al. 2009, Karapanos et al. 2009, Lindley et al. 2009, Rowland et al. 2009, Kjeldskov and Paay 2010).

This is not to say that context is a new phenomena appearing on the research agenda with the emergence of *mobile* computing. Context has indeed been an important concept within human-computer interaction and interaction design since the *second wave* or paradigm of HCI (Bødker 2006, Harrison et al. 2007). The first wave of HCI was a mixture of engineering and human factors focusing on optimizing human-machine fit. The second wave was largely based on cognitive science focusing on the simultaneous processing of information in machines and in the human mind, but this also involved a strong focus on the use of interactive computing systems in the context of the workplace. However, as pointed out by Bødker (2006) while there was lot of discussion about the intricate concept of context in second wave HCI, this research achieved little in terms of defining and operationalising it in a way of any real significant value to HCI and interaction design. In the *third wave*, focus has broadened further toward a post PC ubiquitous and pervasive information society where computer technology has spread "from the workplace to our homes and everyday lives and culture" (Bødker 2006). This means that context is now an *elemental* concept that we not only need to *define* well, but also need to *understand* better in terms of its complexity, significance, and influence on peoples' experience of technology in use, in order to inform technology design better.

Mobile interaction design is positioned in the third wave of HCI. It grew out of the second wave, but the tremendous uptake of mobile computing by the general population subsequently played a contributing factor in the creation, force, and velocity of the third wave by enabling some of the completely new potentials and patterns of computing technology use that we are witnessing globally today.

CHAPTER 3

Design Approaches

As I have allured to a number of times in the previous sections, mobile interaction design is, broadly speaking, characterized by two different approaches to design: a user- and a technology-centered one. This duality reflects the field's strong roots in the discipline of human-computer interaction on one side, and computing on the other, and an associated difference in primary interest amongst researchers and designers in *people* or in *systems*.

3.1 USER-CENTERED DESIGN

User-centered design (UCD) is a design philosophy and overall methodological framework for conceiving interactive systems, which can be traced back to Henry Dreyfuss' 1955 book *Designing for People* (Dreyfuss 1955). It is about designing interactive computer systems from the user's point of view emphasising people rather than technology (Norman and Draper 1986), and it does this by discovering unmet user needs and responding to these through design. Traditionally, user-centered design and research follows an iterative cycle that consists of the four central stages of studying, designing, building, and evaluating interactive systems (cf. Preece et al. 2002, Sharp et al. 2007, Harper et al. 2008). The strengths of this framework is that it is simple, captures some of the essential components of an interaction design process, and provides an overall structure of how to organize them in relation to each other. Historically, another strength of the model has been that it promotes an iterative "prototyping" approach to systems development rather than a linear "waterfall" approach.

The user-centered design philosophy has several branches of more specific methods and associated philosophical views on people and design, such as Participatory Design (PD), Usability Engineering (UE), and Contextual Design (CD). Participatory Design (see, for example, Ehn and Kyng 1987, Bødker 2006, Kensing and Blomberg 1998) has its roots in Scandinavia where it was developed as "Cooperative Design" as a part of several research projects in systems development in collaboration with trade unions dating back to the 1970's and 1980's (see, for example, Bødker et al. 1987, Ehn and Kyng 1991). Participatory Design puts particular emphasis on the active involvement of users, and other stakeholders, in the design process in order to ensure the usefulness of the produced outcomes. This is typically done through an action research process where researchers/designers and users cooperate closely and iteratively, and both gain from the relationship. Participatory Design has a clear underlying political dimension of emancipation and democratization, and can as such be described as one of the more radical human-oriented approaches within user-centered design. Some of the key principles of Participatory Design are that users of technology should be respected as experts in their own domain, and recognized as prime sources of innovation. The design task is approached broadly with focus on people, practices, and technology embedded in specific organizational contexts. As a consequence of this, Participatory Design is heavily field based, with researchers and designers spending significant amounts of time "in the wild" rather than in the lab.

While Participatory Design takes user involvement very seriously and elevates user needs, satisfaction and human well being far beyond anything else, a key critique of this form of user-centered design is that it leads only to incremental design improvements grounded in current practice rather than to design leaps that can facilitate the formation of new practices. The essential reason for this is that users are not necessarily good designers. They are experts in their own domains, and possess important knowledge for informing design, but they usually know very little about technology and design, and are not trained in projecting into the future and envisioning new technologies and designs. This, it can be argued, is better done within the expertise of trained designers or engineers. As described by Jakob Nielsen, "users are not designers, so it is not reasonable to expect them to come up with design ideas from scratch. However, they are very good at reacting to concrete designs they do not like or that will not work in practice" (Nielsen 1993, p. 88-89).

This perspective on the role of users in user-centered design is fundamental to the Usability Engineering approach (see, for example, Nielsen 1993, Preece et al. 1993, Spool et al. 1999, Rosson and Caroll 2001). Usability Engineering emerged as a distinct area of research and practice in the mid to late 1980's. As indicted by its name, it originates from the more engineering-oriented parts of human-computer interaction with many usability engineering researchers and practitioners having a background in either computer science or a sub-area of psychology such as perception, cognition or human factors. Usability engineering emphasizes the making of user interfaces with high usability or user friendliness as defined by, for example, the ISO 9241 standard about the effectiveness, efficiency and satisfaction with which specified users achieve specified goals in a specified context of use. This is done by iterating through phases of user requirements gathering, prototype development and usability evaluation against a set of quality metrics. Evaluation is done either by usability experts through, for example, heuristic inspection (Nielsen and Molich 1990) or by testing systems with users (Rubin 1994). Although field-based usability testing has been given some attention, usability engineering is heavily laboratory based, with researchers and practitioners spending most of their time in controlled environments rather than in the wild—even when testing mobile computing devices and applications (see for, example, Weiss 2002).

Although usability engineering implies user involvement, a key criticism of this approach is that it reduces the roles of these users to being informants for requirements and test subjects for designs. Consequently, they are typically far removed from the actual design and development process, and only brought in very early in the process, before any design has been done, and/or very late when many design decisions have already been made. Another critique of usability engineering in relation to interaction design is that it focuses too exclusively on one particular quality of a design—its usability—and on assessing and making recommendations about where to improve this, rather than on the broader user experience of the design, in all of its contextual complexity, and facilitating the creation of life- and work-enhancing interaction design matching this context.

In an attempt to overcome some of these limitations, Contextual Design seeks to broaden the perspective of the usability engineering process to explicitly include the context, and to inform design more strongly rather than merely assessing and, sometimes, providing recommendations for redesign. Contextual Design is a specific method within the user-centered design philosophy developed by Beyer and Holtzblatt (1998) that accommodates field studies in system development by combining ethnographic methods for data gathering relevant to a particular product, rationalizing workflows, and designing human-computer interfaces. Although parts of the method can fruitfully be applied to non-work-related domains, the contextual design method is in essence about supporting work activities through structured and contextually grounded user-centered design. To put it bluntly, it is not a method of interaction design but a good method for doing user-centered usability engineering. Contextual Design provides a detailed account for what exactly to do, when and how, in a user-centered design process. It does, however, not provide an overall framework for integrating the different disciplines of interaction design. Although it has a strong component of fieldwork and contextual analysis of work and organizations, it is weaker in terms of supporting design and evaluation. Both of these are approached as activities of usability engineering. Contextual Design also doesn't integrate well the technical aspects of interaction design in working with actual technology and prototypes. On the positive side, one of the absolute strengths of Contextual Design is that it is very solution oriented, which makes it attractive as a methodological foundation in industry and research organizations doing more solution-oriented ICT work. It does, however, not provide a strong foundation for doing academic research, as it does not address or support the need for creating theoretically grounded understandings of the domain in focus or the solutions developed as a part of the design process.

3.2   TECHNOLOGY-DRIVEN DESIGN

Contrasting the user-centered approach, another overall philosophy is to let *technology* drive the process of design. Technology-driven design is about letting the possibilities of new technologies, or existing ones in new combinations, inform what we design and build. Put on the edge, technology-driven designs are not solutions to problems expressed by users but instead solutions to technical problems looking for possible use. They are propositions envisioned by designers or researchers based on their knowledge of what can be done, and not in response to what people or users have asked for. In his provocative and highly debated March 2010 column of the ACM Interactions magazine "Technology First, Needs Last," Donald Norman argues that technology-driven design is invariably responsible for all conceptual breakthroughs in modern history. Grand inventions, such as flush toilets, plumbing, electric lighting, cars, airplanes, and ICT, Norman argues, happen because they have been made possible technologically, and not because people have asked for them or necessarily needed them beforehand. Technologists create new designs *because they can*. Products, applications, use, and especially *needs*, evolve slowly afterwards (Norman 2010).

Technology-driven design is inherently a trial-and-error based approach in which new ideas are developed, tested, and then explored further or scrapped. Methodologically this makes it a risky and time consuming approach relying on the team's capabilities of reasoning through intuition, experience, deduction, and induction with no guarantee of any useful outcome or solution being produced (Kjeldskov and Graham 2003, Danis and Karat 1995). On the other hand, however, this fundamental reliance on the competence of the researchers and designers strongly facilitates the utilization of the precious source of creativity and innovation that these exact people represent. They are typically experts in their area of technology and therefore able to look beyond the technological horizon that "users" without this insight normally have.

Although not a formally established paradigm (like user-centered design), technology-driven design has always been implicitly present as a fundamental approach within the area of computing. According to van den Ende and Dolfsma (2004), neither the development of digital computers after 1960 nor the convergence of computing and communication technologies after 1990 can be explained by rising demand or newly discovered user needs or demands. Instead, it was the development of new technological knowledge that was the enabler of new types of computers such as the PC and new communication applications such as the Internet. Had this knowledge been available earlier, those technologies would most likely have been developed and adopted then. Hence, just like any other area of technology, computing has partly emerged and evolved through a process of technology-driven design based on an interest to explore what would be technically possible more than what would be useful to do. This is simply an established way of doing research within an emerging area of technology (Kjeldskov 2003). Before we can begin contemplating broader phenomena like use, usability, and user experiences of new technology, this technology simply needs to be available in some concrete and functioning form. Technology-driven design provides this, and should therefore not be ignored as a driver, or enabler, of interaction design. On the contrary, one could argue that it is in fact a necessary precondition for user-centered design.

Faced with progress where processing power has increased exponentially for half a century, and networking capability, display technology and input devices also follow a significantly fast paced evolution, Jones and Marsden (2006) argue that it is very hard *not* to let technology drive the development of interactive mobile systems and devices. They argue that while user-centered design approaches stay clear of thinking about technology until the user needs have been identified and described—in order not to be distracted by detailed design consideration—when designing mobile interactions there appear to be advantages in allowing the potentials of technology to play a more central role in the process. This view is shared by Rogers et al. (2002) who argue that looking at technologies themselves can be a valuable source of inspiration for design, and by Danis and Karat (1995) who argue that technology-driven design facilitates a dual goal of advancing technology *as well* as creating new usage benefits, while user-centered design primarily focus only on the latter. In the latest issue of ACM Interactions, the importance of technology-driven research is also addressed by Kritina Höök, arguing that it is time for the CHI community to reconnect with the potentials of emerging technologies and, as in the past, "shape interactions based on a deep, well-cultivated understanding of technological capacities" (Höök 2012).

3.3   AT THE INTERSECTION BETWEEN USERS AND TECHNOLOGY

In light of the discussion above, if we choose to see interaction design as a matter of innovating and creating new ways of using technology, one can argue that a central shortcoming of the UCD approach is its strong focus on users. Undoubtedly, hearing such a statement from an HCI research academic is bound to cause some raised eyebrows, but bear with me here. Over the last couple of years it has become more and more evident that some companies, most notably Apple, are able to develop, produce, and sell millions of novel interactive computer products with groundbreaking interaction design, high utility and usability, and premium user experiences *without* following a user-centered design approach as prescribed by our primary textbooks. How is this possible? *What is it that those companies do that is missing from the established literature on the topic?* It appears to me that the problem originates in UCD being so good at grounding the interaction design task in *current practice* that it impedes our ability to break free from this and imagine *future practices* that are fundamentally different. User-centered design focuses on discovering unmet user needs, but in successfully doing so these needs are reinforced rather than questioned and challenged.

As a consequence, UCD has a track record of resulting in small incremental improvements rather than in fundamental breakthroughs or radical new inventions (Verganti 2010). As discussed by Norman (2010), such improvements are often highly valuable, and in fact, where the most frequent gains come from, *but* this type of value adding is very different from the "success by innovation" that prompted the initial questions above. Contrasting the incremental improvements facilitated by, for example, UCD, Norman continues to argue that conceptual breakthroughs are driven exclusively by new inventions in technology in response to which user needs arise much later. His examples are many, including the automobile, airplane, radio, TV, computer, and, of course, mobile phones. Although I agree with Donald Norman about the shortcomings of UCD raised in his column, I do not agree with the conclusion that we should "leave it to the technologists" to "get the grand ideas running." In fact, Normans own examples of new technology initially failing until someone other than the inventor comes along and envisions new usage indicates to me that there is something else at play here. Instead, I believe that what we are looking for lies in the middle ground between the two. Between fundamental technology invention and incremental user-centered development, or "at the intersection between technology and liberal arts" (Jobs 2010) as often illustrated by Steve Jobs in the later years (Figure 3.1). What we are looking for is exactly what

Norman (2010) does not extract from his own examples: the radical innovation created by *merging new technological possibilities with visions of future practice*—without asking the users what they want, but by making radical proposals about it.

Figure 3.1: Steve Jobs on Apple's success at designing interactive products: "We've always tried to be at the intersection of technology and liberal arts, to be able to get the best of both, to make extremely advanced products from a technology point of view, but also have them be intuitive, easy to use, fun to use, so that they really fit the users—the users don't have to come to them, they come to the user" (Jobs 2010).

This is precisely what companies like Apple are good at doing. In Apple's innovation process "insights do not move from users to Apple but the other way around. More than Apple listening to us, it's us who listen to Apple" (Verganti 2010). However, these radical proposals are not created by chance or from intuition of a visionary guru but from very precise processes and capabilities (Verganti 2009). They require a solid understanding of both technology and of users—perhaps even understanding users more than they understand themselves—and for the latter some of the techniques used within UCD, such as ethnographic studies, are still valuable. Not "to discover hidden, unmet needs" (Norman 2010) but to deeply understand the context that we are designing for.

CHAPTER 4

A Decade of Mobile HCI Research

My own research in interaction design for mobile computers began in 2001. At that time, Mobile HCI and interaction design research was still very much in its infancy as an academic research area. Widely commercially successful devices had only been around for about a decade, and leading conferences had only a few years of history behind them. As a consequence only a small body of knowledge existed about this emerging research field in terms of methodology, interaction design, and real world use, and no coherent sets of methods and techniques for mobile interaction design had yet been established. Driven by the saturation and technological maturity of mobile devices throughout society, there was, however, a huge interest in the new interaction design possibilities of this fast expanding area of computing. This situation motivated me to carry out a comprehensive literature survey of mobile interaction design research. The purpose of this was to provide a snapshot of state-of-the-art and current practices, and through this identify shortcomings and opportunities for future research directions.

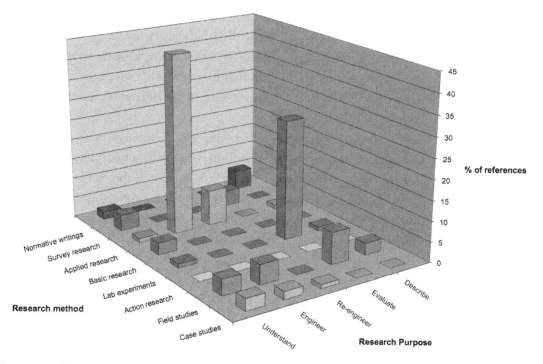

Figure 4.1: Mobile interaction design research methods and purposes (2000-2002).

In that paper, we reviewed 102 articles published between 2000-2002 in the most central outlets of its time and classified them in terms of their research method and purpose, as described in Table 4.1 (inspired by Wynekoop and Conger 1990). This provided a picture of how mobile interaction design research was being done, and for what intent, and brought to attention a number of trends characterizing the field, and a number of assumptions influencing its focus and approach. The distribution of articles on research methods and purpose is illustrated in Figure 4.1 clearly showing two peaks, a number of notable but less frequent groupings, and a large number of gaps.

Table 4.1: Overview of research methods and purposes	
Method	
Case studies	Intensive empirical investigations of contemporary phenomena within small size entities such as groups, organizations, individuals, systems, or tools in real-life context with the researcher distinct from the phenomena being studied
Field studies	Characterized by taking place in "the real world" covering a range of qualitative and quantitative approaches from ethnographic studies of phenomena in their social and cultural context to field experiments in which a number of independent variables are manipulated
Action research	A method through which researchers not only add to the body of scientific knowledge but also apply that knowledge to the object of interest through intervention and participation in the activity being studied
Lab experiments	Characterized by taking place in a controlled environment created for the purpose of research or in dedicated laboratories allowing a detailed focus on specific phenomena of interest with a large degree of experimental control
Survey research	Informs research gathers large amounts of data through various techniques such as questionnaires and interviews from a known sample of selected respondents assumed to be independent of their environment
Applied research	Builds on trial and error on the basis of reasoning through intuition, experience, deduction, and induction. Typically, the desired outcome of an applied research process is known while means of accomplishing it is not. This makes applied research very goal oriented
Basic research	Characterized by trial-and-error-based development of new theories and the study of well-known problems to which neither solutions nor methods are known, relying on the competences of the researcher

Normative writings	Cover the body of "non-research" writings about phenomena of interests such as concept development writings organizing ideas for stimulating future research, presentation of truth describing ideas that seem intuitively correct, and descriptions of applications
Purpose	
Understanding	The purpose of research focusing on finding the meaning of studied phenomena through, for example, frameworks or theories developed from collected data
Engineering	The purpose of research focused toward developing new systems or parts of systems, for example an interaction technique for a mobile device, or a mobile application or device
Re-engineering	The purpose of research focusing on improving existing systems by re-developing them such as, for example, adapting a web browser to a small display
Evaluating	The purpose of research assessing or validating products, theories, or methods, for example, the usability or user experience of a specific application, or a theory of interaction
Describing	The purpose of research focusing on defining desirable properties of products, for example, an interactive mobile guide system, or mobile interaction design method

4.1   TRENDS AND ASSUMPTIONS

The literature survey revealed a strong bias toward applied research for engineering and laboratory experiments for evaluation, as shown in Figure 3.2. Put simply, mobile interaction design research in the early 2000's was dominated by building new systems in a trial-and-error manner, and evaluating them in laboratory settings—if evaluating them at all. There was very little going on in terms of trying to understand the phenomenon of mobility itself in relation to interaction design and technology use, and to use such insight when designing and building actual interactive systems. Nor was much attention given to the role of real-world context in relation to understanding, building, or evaluating interactive mobile systems (Kjeldskov and Graham 2003). In essence this echoed a fundamental segregation between use- and technology-centeredness depending on whether the involved researchers were primarily interested in *people* or *systems*. On a more general level, it became apparent that methodology seemingly played a very small role. The approaches taken often remained unexplained, their suitability unchallenged, and their limitations and alternatives not discussed.

Based on our more detailed analysis of what types of research and purposes were missing, or largely underrepresented, we cautioned that the bias toward trial-and-error building of interactive systems, evaluations only in the lab, and the lack of research for understanding design and use in real world contexts, would limit the quality and scope of the body of knowledge about mobile human-computer interaction being accumulated, and thereby inhibit the advancement and impact of the research field in the future. In particular we found three underlying, and unfortunate, assumptions at the time—namely that appeared that:

1. we already knew what to build;

2. context was not important; and

3. methodology mattered very little.

In the following I will briefly take a critical look at these three assumptions and their potential implication for research.

4.1.1   DID WE ALREADY KNOW WHAT TO BUILD?

The prevalent approach of applied research for engineering indicated an assumption at the time that we already knew what systems to build and what problems to solve, such as limited screen real estate, limited means for interaction, and limited network bandwidth. We just didn't know yet exactly how to build these systems and how to solve those problems, but the solutions existed out there and were just waiting to be uncovered. Only very little research addressed the more fundamental questions of what is useful and what is perceived problematic from a user-perspective, and evaluations focused on functionality rather than context-centered and user-centered issues. Given the young age of the research field we argued that this could hardly be true and that, on the contrary, young emerging research fields such as this particularly require research addressing such fundamental issues. Continuing to do research on the basis of the assumption that we already know the problem would, in it self, make it very difficult to set this assumption aside and identify the more fundamental challenges at hand.

4.1.2   WAS CONTEXT NOT IMPORTANT?

The limited focus on real-world studies indicated an assumption that context was not really important for what we build, and that interactive mobile computer systems are by definition suitable solutions. Building and evaluating interactive systems on the basis of applied research and laboratory experiments also results in very concrete conclusions about very specific solutions. These conclusions can be difficult to generalize and therefore it can be difficult to elevate our learning from the systems we develop, and study in use, to an abstract level where knowledge can be transferred to other design cases, technologies, domains, users, purposes, etc. This limits the research field's ability to move forward at a pace beyond incremental steps from one specific design to the next. Hence, in our opinion, the assumption, that building and evaluating systems by trial and error is better than grounding engineering, evaluation, and theory in user-based studies, seriously weakened the mobile HCI and interaction design research field at the time.

4.1.3   DID METHODOLOGY MATTER VERY LITTLE?

The observation that only very few studies were based on an explicitly described and considered methodological foundation indicated an assumption that methodology mattered very little in mobile HCI and interaction design research. We presented this supposition as a particularly problematic one because it is well known that the choice of method clearly influences the results subsequently produced (Myers 1997). Problem solving by applied research is, for example, often viewed as a rather poor method because it demands huge efforts by researchers and often "translates into poor performance because they require search of a large space of possibilities" (Wynekoop and Conger 1990). In relation to mobile interaction design research, a lack of fundamental critical reflection on methodology, and sensitivity to its importance, would impede our ability to identify limitations of our work and inhibit the breakthroughs in design and use discovered through deliberately looking at and doing things different than previously.

4.1.4   OPPORTUNITIES

Part of the reason for the bias toward applied research for engineering combined with laboratory experiments for evaluation is that this is a natural place to start when exploring a new field of emerging technology. Before we can study and understand phenomena like use contexts, usability, and user experiences of new technology, we need this technology to be available to us in some concrete and functioning form. However, if a field of *emerging* technology is to evolve into a field of *applied* technology, it is important not to get stuck in research methodologies where solutions are created and put to use by trial-and-error rather than grounded in real world context. Another part of the reason, I believe, is that rather than mobile technologies not being ready for studies in natural settings, the body of mobile HCI research and researchers were not really ready for natural settings research. In the early 2000's only very few studies had been published that used natural setting research methods within mobile HCI and interaction design. Consequently, only very few examples existed for others to be inspired by and follow, and the whole debate about doing research slightly differently had not even started. Adding to this, it was still very unclear exactly how to make use of methods like field studies, case studies, and action research in mobile HCI and interaction design, and what value they might bring to a specific project. Hence, in the early 2000's the multi-disciplinarity of mobile HCI and interaction design was not yet strong. Like other areas of emerging computing technologies it was very much a technical research area dominated by electrical engineering and computer science. In terms of methodology this meant that methods and techniques from, for example, social science, the humanities, and the arts naturally did not yet have a strong presence in the minds and traditions of the dominant mobile HCI researchers at the time, and dominant researchers from those adjacent fields were not yet working with mobile HCI and interaction design themselves.

Apart from describing and discussing current practice in mobile interaction design research, the survey also outlined a variety of opportunities for doing future research methodologically differently. In particular, the noticeable lack of *field studies* presented an obvious opportunity to use this method for exploring rich real-world use cases, contexts, and user needs to gain deeper understanding of these. As a particular approach, we suggested that learning from other disciplines that have struggled with the study of similar "slippery" phenomena, such as ethnography, could provide important methodological insight. We also proposed that field studies within mobile HCI and interaction design should be used to inform the engineering of new designs, and the re-engineering of existing ones, through context-centered and user-centered identification of needs and opportunities for innovation. Finally, in response to the bias toward evaluating in laboratory settings, we promoted the opportunity for systematic investigation of field studies for this purpose, as mobility and context can be difficult to emulate in a laboratory.

The clear lack of *survey* and *case study* research also presented huge opportunities. In the field of Information Systems, for example, these approaches are used widely to collect large amounts of data from, for example, a large segment of actual end-users of an interactive system, enabling much greater power of generalization. Case studies within mobile HCI and interaction design could increase learning from existing interactive systems within real-world contexts. Such case studies would enable close scrutiny of specific phenomena in specific settings, which could then be used to enrich the collective knowledge in the discipline and to enable key issues to be described and understood. The issues generated could then be used to generate hypotheses to propagate further research. The very limited amount of *basic research* indicated an opportunity for the development of theoretical frameworks, and application of existing ones from other disciplines, for describing and understanding mobile interaction design and use. Finally, we argued that the complete absence of *action research* pointed to both the lack of a well-established body of theoretical research within the discipline and the unwillingness to implement mobile systems uncertain to succeed and taking a long time to implement and evaluate. This was perhaps not surprising, given the cost of such technology and the associated implementation overhead at the time. Nonetheless, studies of practice and intervention were, again, an opportunity to develop new kinds of knowledge in the discipline.

Only a few years after the literature survey, mobile interaction design research had already started to change. The methodological opportunities proposed were indeed taken up by a lot of our colleagues, and today, a decade later, the research field has matured considerably and is making use of a much wider palette of research methods in interesting combinations, and for a much wider range of purposes. This trend was confirmed by a follow-up survey reviewing all research articles concerning the design of mobile interactions published in top outlets in 2009 (Kjeldskov and Paay 2012). From this survey it was apparent that the research field of mobile interaction design had grown substantially in the last decade and is now a substantial part of mainstream HCI and interaction design research. Out of the 246 full and short papers in the Proceedings of the Annual ACM Conference on Human Factors in Computing Systems (CHI) that year, almost a fifth concerned human-computer interaction with mobile systems or devices. It is also clear that there has been an increase in the level of empirical research, and that a more diversified set of methodologies for this has evolved. For example, the use of *field studies* have notably changed and diversified into at least three noteworthy sub categories of *field ethnographies*, *field experiments*, and *field surveys*.

At the same time, however, there is also clear evidence that the underlying segregation into camps primarily interested in *people* or in *systems* persists. The first aims primarily at understanding mobile user experiences theoretically and conceptually, and the second aims primarily at building new mobile systems and evaluating them in use. This segregation of course stems from the multi-disciplinarity of the research field, but maintaining such a divide sadly sustains the unfortunate implicit assumption that in mobile interaction design research people and technology can, or perhaps even *should*, be studied separately. In turn, such an assumption can be partially responsible for researchers in the people- and technology- oriented camps continuing to investigate the same types of questions and problems as before, rather than defining and exploring new ones in closer collaboration. Within both approaches *users* play an important role, but in the first they are the *objects* of the research, while in the second they are research *subjects*. According to Rasmussen (2007), such clear-cut distinction tends to cause the potentially fruitful dialectics between the two approaches to disappear. If one of the two approaches is considered 100% good and the other 100% bad, from either side of the divide, then one is destined to subsume the other. Dialectic thinking, on the other hand, encourages us to develop a synthesis at a higher stage of the opposing interests, as also discussed by Dahlbom and Mathiassen (1993). This is not simply a matter of finding a balance between the two but about transcending beyond opposing views and shaping a new unity at another level (Nonaka and Toyama 2002). Hence, in order to continue informing the creation of better interactive mobile devices and systems, a closer integration of these two approaches, the user- and the technology-centered one, is still needed.

4.2   EMERGING CHALLENGES

In light of the developments in mobile interaction design research over the last decade, what then are the challenges emerging today? As I described in the Introduction, it is my opinion that the enormous uptake of mobile devices, and the role that they have come to play in our lives, means that mobile computing has evolved from being strongly an engineering profession to being, at least, equally strongly a design profession. Hence, interaction design is today of greater importance for the continuing development of mobile computing than ever before, and there is a need to ensure that our overall approaches to the way that we think about and design mobile interactions are up for the challenges that lay ahead. In order to do this I argue that we may benefit from exploring, more profoundly, *designerly ways* of thinking and doing, and from widening our scope, more significantly, to look at the contextual user experience of interactive mobile systems and devices and the digital ecosystems they are forming.

In my view, the first emerging challenge for designing mobile interactions is to *transcend beyond the dichotomy of people- or technology-oriented research and design*. Continuing such divide we are at risk of missing the holistic nature of the mobile interaction design challenges currently at hand, as mobile technologies have matured considerably and now pervade almost every aspect of our lives. What is instead needed is to "reconceptualize the domain of interest through using a modified unit of analysis" (Rogers et al. 2005)—creating a shift in focus where new and shared problems are framed in a way that force new ways of thinking and operating, while still allowing the use of existing concepts and theory. The second emerging challenge is to *widen the scope beyond the individual mobile device and an individual user's interaction with it*. This initial perspective has been researched in depth for over a decade, in both artificial and natural settings, and is now understood quite well. What is *not* understood very well is mobile interaction design within the even larger context, or wholeness, of everyday life and the use of other technologies, that interactive mobile systems have become a part of.

As I will discuss in the next chapter, transcending beyond people and technology, and widening the scope beyond devices and users, may be achieved by changing the way we think about and do interaction design, from a scientific way toward a designerly way.

CHAPTER 5

Toward a Designerly Way

I will now shift focus from reviewing past mobile interaction design practice and research to discussing how we can facilitate that these continue to be carried out with significance and impact in the future. In this chapter I will draw on design research literature from outside the field of interaction design, and show how a synthesis of these thoughts and concepts can help enrich the way we think about and design mobile interactions today.

I am going to start by discussing the need for doing, and thinking about, interaction design in a *designerly way* rather than in a traditional scientific way. This is not just a matter of wording or branding, but involves some profound changes to the underlying philosophy, approach, reasoning, and focus in interaction design as a profession and research area. For this purpose I will discuss four different perspectives on design and introduce *contextualism* as an alternative, constructivistic, worldview to the, essentially positivistic, ones still pervading large parts of mobile interaction design today. I will also illustrate how contextual views have informed information systems research, and shaped modern architecture and architectural theory in ways that can enrich our thinking about interaction design. Finally, I will revisit the user-centered design (UCD) approach in light of introduced concepts and perspectives, and elaborate on this model toward a contextual approach focusing on the continual convergence of form and context.

5.1 FROM TECHNICAL RATIONALITY TO CONTINUAL CONVERGENCE

While mobile interaction design is a relatively young field of study, *design* has been a recognizable topic of research since the early 1960's. The area of "Design Research" promotes "the study of and research into the process of designing in all its many fields" (Design Research Society 1966), and has had a strong presence within the research area of Information Systems dating back to the early 1980's. Surprisingly, however, given its seemingly obvious relevance, Design Research has only had very small presence in interaction design—and even less in *mobile* interaction design. Notable exceptions include the work of Rogers (2004), Buxton (2007), Moggridge (2007), and Stolterman (2008).

Design Research has in itself undergone an interesting evolution in philosophy, approach, and focus over the last 50 years, and some of the thinking about design that it has spawned can be used to frame and indicate possible ways forward within the design of mobile interactions. In brief, the origins leading to Design Research can be traced back to early 1920's movements of modern design based on values of objectivity and rationality. The aspiration to "scientize" design re-emerged in post-World War II's increased interest in the use of "systematic methods of problem solving, borrowed from computer techniques and management theory, for assessment of design problems and development of design solutions" (Archer 1965), leading to the "design methods movement" of the 1960's where objectivity and rationality began being applied to processes and not just products (Cross 2001; de Figueiredo and da Cunha 2007). The underlying assumption of instrumental or technical rationality was that design, like science, can be dealt with through decomposition and systematic search through possible solutions. Prominent work within this approach to design included Herbert Simon's *The Sciences of the Artificial* (Simon 1969), introducing concepts such as "bounded rationality," and even the early work of Christopher Alexander (1964), which had a flavor of rational methodology—although Alexander himself later declared his complete dissociation with this. In the 1970's, however, there was a backlash against the positivistic scientization of design, responding to the seeming inability of technical rationality to "help society achieve its objectives and solve its problems" (Schön 1983), and fueled by the social and political movements of the time rejecting the conservative values underlying it (Cross 2001). The rejection of technical rationality led to renewed vigour in design research in the early 1980's, seeking the development of design as a discipline with epistemology and foundation in its own history of practice rather than in science. This is largely captured in Donald Schön's *The Reflective Practitioner* (1983), which "explicitly challenged the positivist doctrine underlying much of the design science movement" (Cross 2001) but also partly in Nigel Cross' quest for a "designerly" way of knowing, thinking, and acting (Cross 1982).

One of Schön's central messages is that from a technical rationality perspective, professional practice, such as design, is a process of problem *solving*, but that in real world practice problems are not given but need to be constructed. This requires a problem *setting* approach, in which we name what we will attend to and frame its context (Schön 1983 p. 40). In a similar way, Cross argues that there are designerly ways of knowing, thinking and acting, fundamentally different from the generally recognized scientific and scholarly ways, and that these are more about defining the limits of the problem and suggesting the nature of its possible solution, than they are about exhaustive systematic analysis (Cross 1982). This thinking is echoed in a seminal paper by Giovan Lanzara (1983) who outlines three different views on design as: (1) functional analysis, (2) problem-solving, and (3) problem-setting, and argues that understanding the underlying views on design can help explain the problems that constrain it. The first two of these correspond to the technical rationality approach while the third corresponds to Schön's concepts of *reflection in* and *on action*, and partly Cross's *designerly way* of knowing, thinking and acting. In design as *functional analysis*, design is a process of systematically breaking down the problem through rational analysis and thereby revealing the structure of the one optimal solution. In design as *problem-solving*, design is about finding solutions to problems. In doing this the designer can learn how to structure his search and how to proceed to the next step from the context. The solution only needs to be "satisficing" (Simon 1969), and it is known that it is just one of many possibilities. In design as *problem-setting*, design is a process of collective inquiry and search taking place through transactions and conversations among several actors with mixed interests in the problem at hand. What needs to be created is what the problem solving view takes for granted, and problem representations are not context-free but largely context-sensitive (Lanzara 1983). Design, thereby, becomes a reflective conversation with the materials of the situation (Schön 1992, Winograd 1996, ch. 9).

5.1.1   DESIGN AS DEALING WITH EMERGENT GOALS

Extending on the thoughts of Lanzara (1983) and Schön (1983, 1992), Gasson (2006) introduces a fourth view to represent a contemporary understanding of design processes. In design as *emergent evolutionary learning*, design is the continuous convergence of problem-understanding and solution-proposition through a cyclical process of learning about a situation and responding through design that is deliberately short-term and partial. This view resonates strongly with Schön's later notion of design as a continual reflective conversation with materials (Schön 1992, Winograd 1996) but emphasizes to a larger degree than Schön the dynamic and emergent nature of the *context and goals* of a design and not only of the design itself. The process of design is still rooted in a process of collective inquiry and search, but the notion that structure is inherent in a situation, as assumed in design as problem-solving, is explicitly rejected. Instead, contexts are seen as inherently dynamic and evolving, hence requiring design to be a continuously evolving process too, with an ongoing focus on *both* changing form and changing context. Not only are the problems unclear at the start of the process, so are the *goals* of the design (de Figueiredo and da Cunha 2007). However, as partial solutions are explored, an understanding of the problems, and appropriate design goals, emerges (Gasson 2006).

The view on design as dealing with emergent goals captures, to a large degree, the essence of Christopher Alexander's most recent work on *The Nature of Order* (2002–2005). Here, Alexander goes a step beyond the participatory and reflective approach outlined in *A Pattern Language* (Alexander et al. 1977) and *The Timeless Way of Building* (Alexander 1979), and promotes a holistic process of design unfolding where both the context and the form are continuously evolving through a step-by-step morphogenetic process of *wholeness-extending transformations*, that are each intentionally short and open ended. The central contribution of this work of Alexander's in relation to Simon (1969) and Schön (1983) is, in my opinion, that it helps transcend the whole notion of a "problem," and instead makes us focus on the "desiderata," or "that-which-is-desired" (Nelson and Stolterman 2003) in the broader facilitation of human life in all its aspects and richness. Rather than setting and solving problems, Alexander's wholeness-extending design view allows us to treat design as a matter of creating new desired practice, and of dealing with the sometimes ill-defined goals emerging from the design process itself. It may set and solve a problem, but it may also just enable humans to do activities that they couldn't do before—on smaller or larger scales of importance for their life —like streaming a movie or photo from their mobile to their TV, or seeing on their mobile what friends and family on a different continent are up to at the moment. These are interactions that are hard to describe well as "solutions to problems" but easy to describe as meaningful and desirable extensions of a wholeness that was already there.

The notions of wholeness extending transformations, and emergent evolutionary learning both reflect an evolution of the design discipline over the last three decades, in correspondence with a larger shift in society's world-view from one of positivism toward one of constructivism (de Figueiredo and da Cunha 2007, Alvarez and Kilbourne 2002). This evolution of design and shift in world view is of particular interest for contemporary research in the design of mobile interactions because it has parallels with the shift in focus beyond an individual user's interaction with an individual device for a well defined activity, toward the wholeness of mobile technology user experience in indefinable and unbounded activities within the larger, and dynamic, contexts of emergent everyday life.

Looking critically at the predominant design approaches within the area of human-computer interaction, discussed in Chapter 3, one could argue that these all fall within Lanzara's three design views, and none of them within the emerging holistic perspective. User-centered design in the form of usability engineering and contextual design are essentially about problem-solving as descried by Lanzara (1983). It is about developing simplified models of the real world, and thereby "bounding" the problem until it becomes sufficiently well defined to be resolved. Solving the problem is then done by evaluating alternative solutions until one that fulfils a set of criteria is discovered. Hence, design is a rational search process, and solutions are never considered universally optimal, but merely "satisficing" (Simon 1969). The participatory design methodology is different from the usability engineering and Contextual Design approaches to user-centered design in that it particularly addresses the problem-setting aspect of design, or at least aims to do so. Corresponding to Lanzara's (1983) collective inquiry through transactions and conversations among several actors with mixed interests, Participatory Design assumes that there are different perspectives on what the problem is and how it should be solved (Bratteteig 2007), and seeks to uncover these through active involvement of users and other stakeholders in the design process. Hence, design is a reflective conversation with the situation (Schön 1983, 1992), and solutions are unique and appropriate. They are shaped by the shaping of the situation.

Technology-centered design can to some degree be described as functional-analysis in that complexity is reduced by applying scientific reductionism to the (technical) problem at hand. However, in light of Simon's (1969) notions of bounded rationality, rejecting the idea of one rationally optimal solution, it is fairer to describe most technology-centered design as matters of problem-solving. Like usability engineering it is about reducing, or "bounding," the problem by taking ill-structured problems and reducing them into well-structured ones through inductive abstraction, rather than rational decomposition, and then exploring a range of possible solutions essentially through a process of trial-and-error. Unlike usability engineering, however, the initial ill-defined problems are not related to the use of technology, but to the functioning of it.

5.1.2   DESIGN AS CONTINUAL CONVERGENCE

What are then really missing from the current palette of design methodologies in interaction design are approaches corresponding to Alexander's (2002–2005) view on design as wholeness-extending. Such "post–Simon" and "post–Schön" design approaches would take a step further and explicitly subscribe to the view that most activities are unbounded and situated in dynamic contexts, and that the relationship between context and form is therefore a continually changing one requiring that design is inherently cyclic, able to deal with emergent and changing goals, and about construction of context as well as form. They would retain the concepts of "satisficing" design from Simon (1969), although viewed as a much more ephemeral quality, and design as reflection-in-action from Schön (1983), but with added emphasis on designing-through-doing and explicit cyclic exploration of partial solutions as ways of converging requirements and solutions. Rather than a rational *scientized* way of interaction design, this would truly be a *designerly* way: rhetorical, exploratory, emergent, opportunistic, abductive, reflective, ambiguous, and risky (Cross 1999). True to its own epistemology and practice, and justified by the efficacy of its results rather than the rigor of its methods (Archer 1992).

Instead of emergent evolutionary learning I will express such a design approach as one of *continual convergence* of form and context, and claim that apart from also being increasingly problem-setting, rather than merely problem-solving, *mobile interaction design should embrace a designerly way of dealing with dynamic contexts and continuously emergent goals and forms.* In my use of the term "form," as discussed earlier, like Alexander (1964) I refer to the unity of *shape*, *look*, *function*, and *content* that is formed through design. To extend on the line of thought by Greenbaum and Mathiassen (1990), there is nothing wrong with setting and solving problems when designing mobile interactions. But a focus on the continual convergence of form and context helps shift emphasis toward the larger organic wholes, or digital ecosystems if you will, that interactive mobile systems and services have become a part of.

5.2   WORLD VIEWS, ROOT METAPHORS, AND MODES OF INFERENCE

The four views on design as *functional analysis*, *problem-solving*, *problem-setting*, and *continual convergence of form and context* described above, and the shift from technical rationality to reflective practice, or even artistry, can be further conceptualised and understood by applying the theoretical lens of philosopher Stephen Pepper (1942).

According to Pepper (1942) there are four distinct world-views, or root metaphors, through which we can understand the world: *formism*, *mechanism*, *organicism*, and *contextualism*. The root metaphor of formism is similarity. Taking a formist view, we seek to understand what the world *is like* by identifying similarities and differences between things and placing them into meaningful categories. Formist analysis describes either the similarity or differences between two objects, or describes the form that an object exemplifies. The root metaphor of mechanism is the machine. Taking a mechanist view we seek to understand *how things work*. It is assumed that the whole is equal to the sum of the parts, and we try to understand how it works by decomposing complexity into individual parts and looking for cause and effect. Organicism's root metaphor is organic development. The organic perspective is concerned with the coherence between the parts and the whole and tries to understand *how it develops*. Unlike mechanism, organicism does not consider the whole to be simply the sum of the parts, but views the whole as primary and individual parts, only meaningful in relation to this whole. Instability is an inherent characteristic of an organic system. Thus, change is given, and it is stability that needs to be explained. Contextualism, as the last of the four, is based on the root metaphor of act-in-context. Taking a contextual view we are concerned with seeing the world in its complexity of context and the need to continuously adapt to its unpredictability and chance happenings, and seek to understand *how this is happening*. The contextual view sees the world not as forms or machines but as ongoing acts that are inseparable from their history, current context, and threads into the future. Like organicism it views the world holistically, rather than as a sum of individual parts, but it is more pre-occupied with the active present. Looking across these four world-views, formism and mechanism can be described as analytic types of theory (i.e., reductionistic) whereas organicism and contextualism are synthetic (i.e., holistic) types of theory (Pepper 1942). Formism focuses on the concrete, mechanism on laws and principles, organicism on relationships, and contextualism on the contexts in which phenomena occur.

Using Pepper's terms, the shift from viewing design as a matter of functional analysis and problem solving toward a matter of problem setting and continual convergence of form and context is a shift from *formist* and *mechanist* visions of the world to a world-view of *organicism* and *contextualism* (de Figueiredo and da Cunha 2007, p. 66). It is a shift from a reductionistic to a holistic paradigm of design, echoing design research thinking subscribing to the view that the process of solving a design problem is identical with the process of understanding its nature. Similar to dealing with "wicked problems," understanding and resolution of a problem are concomitant (Rittel and Webber 1973, pp. 161-162) and the designer's ideas for solving a problem influences what information is needed to understand it (de Figueiredo and da Cunha 2007, p. 66). Where formism and mechanism, like science, seek to isolative phenomena from the complex situations they are embedded in and extract generalizable principles (Archer 1992), organicism and contextualism, like design, seek to *embrace* complexity and conceive non-universal and "ultimate particular" results (Stolterman 2008, Nelson and Stolterman 2003), purposely embodying a selection of values determined by their context. Applying organicist or contextualist visions to the activity of design, it becomes a matter of viewing the world holistically, looking at the coherence between parts, seeing it in its complexity, and adapting to its unpredictability. Organic and contextual design is perpetual convergences of solutions and problems—continual convergence of form and context.

Pepper (1942) emphasizes that there is a strong tendency to combine contextualist and organicist views, but that there are still some notable differences. Whereas organicism is related to the philosophy of idealism, and explicitly *rejects* reductionism (i.e., formism and mechanism), contextualism is closely related to the philosophy of *pragmatism*, in which positivist principles are accepted, if pragmatically applicable (de Figueiredo and da Cunha 2007). In terms of practice, this means that most non-reductionist design tends to be better characterized as informed by an underlying contextual rather than organicist thinking simply because it typically involves a less rigid—and more pragmatic—view on which principles, techniques, and theories are "allowed" in the design process, as long as it confirms to an overall focus on the contexts in which the design is situated. In pursuit of interdisciplinarity in mobile interaction design, which obviously requires embracing principles, techniques, and theories from other disciplinary areas including ones grounded in positivism, this renders the contextualist (pragmatist) world view most useful.

5.2.1   DESIGN AS ABDUCTIVE THINKING

When taking a contextual approach to design as proposed here, we also implicitly subscribe to the philosophical worldview of pragmatism, and, at least the vibe of, the thoughts of its founding thinkers, such as William James, Charles Sanders Peirce, John Dewey, and George Herbert Mead. Pragmatism is a philosophical tradition concerned with the interplay between theory and practice. Of particular interest for design research, Peirce's work on the logic of science explores the issue of idea generation, and promotes a certain mode of inference for explaining this. According to Peirce, new ideas come into being through "logical leaps of the mind," which reflects a third mode of logical reasoning, different from the more conventional forms of deductive and inductive logic. He named this third form of reasoning *abductive* logic. In abductive reasoning, rather than seeking the effect given the cause and rule, or seeking the rule given the cause and effect, we know the rule and the effect but are looking for the *cause*. Through abductive reasoning we create hypotheses through "inference to the best explanation" (Harman 1965) or guided by our "guessing instinct" (Peirce 1931-1958). Peirce came to this viewpoint through a fascination with the origin of new ideas, and the observation that they arose when thinkers encountered data that didn't fit with established models (Martin 2009). The first step in reasoning from here is not observation but *wondering*, and then imagining what could possibly be true. During this process, new ideas emerge as we collect, combine, and organize our thoughts in different ways.

Looking at the activity of design *in a designerly way*, as discussed above, it is clear that we are dealing with Peirce's world of abduction: actively seeking new data or signs of effect, challenging accepted explanations or rules, and inferring possible new worlds or causes (Martin 2009). Design *is* abductive (Cross 1999, 2011). It is not about predicting an effect or composing a rule. It is about suggesting possible causes (design) that will create an effect given what we know. Rather than trying to deduct "what is," or induct "why something is," designers are seeking to propose "what might be" (Martin 2009).

As discussed by Martin (2009), a fair critique of abductive thinking in design is, of course, that it does not guarantee success but might possibly lead to poor results—which is why it often scares management and others thinking in a non-designerly way. Therefore, abductive thinking in design should not exclude other forms of reasoning, and should not be used as an alibi for basing everything on intuition and guesswork. But at the same time, as pointed out by Cross, design *is* risky (Cross 1999, 2011), and *not* taking risks in design is more likely a guarantee of failure.

With these conceptual foundations in place, and the suggestion to take a contextual approach to designing mobile interactions driven by abductive "leaps of the mind" and designerly ways of knowing, thinking and acting, I will now take a closer look at an area where such thinking has already thrived for some time, namely contextual architecture.

5.3   CONTEXTUAL ARCHITECTURE

As Schön points out, architecture is "perhaps the oldest recognized design profession and, as such, functions as a prototype for design in other professions. If there is a fundamental process underlying the differences among design professions, it is in architecture that we are most likely to find it" (Schön 1983, p. 77). Some movements within modern architecture particularly emphasize the importance of matching buildings to their surroundings. This design philosophy, known as "contextual architecture" (Brolin 1980, Ray 1980, Shane 1976), has given rise to several highly acclaimed buildings around the world praised by their inhabitants for the way they fit naturally with their surroundings. Apart from having a notable effect on its *outcomes*, working within this design philosophy also has some profound impacts on the *process* of design. Architects working closely with the context of their buildings spend significant amounts of time developing and assessing their design *on the building site* rather than at the drawing board in their studio. As an example, it is a well-known fact that the Danish architect Jørn Utzon, who is probably best known for the Sydney Opera House, spent considerable time on building allotments exploring their contextual properties before and during the development of his building designs. In a rare interview he even described how he would sometimes map out the possible location of walls and windows by placing lines of small rocks on the ground, and then walk around imagining the view of the surrounding environment from these as yet un-built rooms. In an account of the works of Alex Popov (a Sydney-based contextual architect and former associate of Utzon) it is described how the result of buildings created with such sensitivity to the way they engage with their surrounding environment is that they do not just fit their context well, they themselves become part of that evolving context (McGillick and Carlstrom 2002).

5.3.1   GENIUS LOCI AND TIMELESSNESS

In architectural theory, contextual architecture is described as a matter of pursuing the notion of *genius loci* (the protective spirit of a place in classical Roman religion) by responding to the topographical, geographical, social, and cultural context of a building site (McGillick and Carlstrom 2002). This concept is most notably explored by Norwegian architect and theorist Christian Norberg-Schulz in his phenomenology of architecture (Norberg-Schulz 1980) arguing that genius loci—or sensitivity to context—has profound implications for place making. Echoing this line of thought, Christopher Alexander argues that architecture exhibiting a quality of "timelessness" always evolves through a series of "wholeness-extending transformations" (Alexander 2007) in which the designer has not only focused on the creation of new form but also done this with deep understanding of and respect for the existing context. Alexander's Pattern Language (Alexander et al. 1977) contains a collection of form-context pairs composed to help evoke the readers' imagination of a future design in context—enabling such wholeness preserving contextual architecture in practice. Such quality of design is also described as "ensoulment" by Nelson and Stolterman (2003, p. 285) who writes that "ensoulment is about wholeness and composition, as well as value and meaning" and that "to ensoul a design—in a way that attracts attention and appreciation—demands a respect for the materials, the structure, the shape and its social dimensions" (i.e., its context).

Over the course of more than four decades of empirical work, Christopher Alexander's view on design has evolved considerably toward a holistic and dynamic perspective of the world, resembling the vertical progression outlined in Table 7.1 From the borderline technical-rationality thinking about the interplay between form and context expressed in *Notes on the Synthesis of Form* (1964), over the participatory and reflective approach outlined in *A Pattern Language* (1977) and *The Timeless Way of Building* (1979), to the continual transformation of wholeness expressed in *The Nature of Order* (2002–2005). Using the terms of Pepper (1942), the bulk of this work is an exemplar of contextual thinking—probably even bordering on organicism in its latest propositions. It reflects a designerly way of thinking and acting dominated by abductive reasoning, deals with the setting of the problem and not just its solution, and it emphasizes that design is about the continuous construction of wholes that amount to more than the sum of their parts. This makes Alexander's thinking particularly relevant for a contextual perspective on designing mobile interactions because it resonates with the emerging need for a perspective transcending user- or technology-centeredness and capable of informing the design of digital ecosystems and holistic user experiences rather than just single devices, systems and interactions.

5.3.2   THE NATURE OF ORDER

Alexander's theory about the nature of order (2002–2005) is a complex piece of design philosophy. In this thinking, design is a matter of pursuing a quality that creates a deep subjective feeling of connectedness in people in its presence, but that we do not have an established name for. Alexander himself calls this quality "life," "wholeness" or "living structures," and argue that the degree of life in things is an objectively observable quality that can be measured empirically. He also argues that the degree of life in things is correlated with the repeated appearance of fifteen empirically identified properties: Levels of scale, strong centers, boundaries, alternating repetition, positive space, good shape, local symmetries, deep interlock and ambiguity, contrast, gradients, roughness, echoes, the void, simplicity and inner calm, and not-separateness. These are seen in human-made design with a holistic quality, but also *in natural systems*, which, Alexander speculates, may be why people respond emotionally and cognitively positive to them when encountered in artifacts. The feeling of life in a natural thing or in a design stems from an experience of *its whole* and not simply from the sum of its parts. In fact, according to Alexander, it is the whole that defines the parts and give them meaning, and not the other way around. "The flower is not *made* from petals. The petals are made from their role and position in the flower" (Alexander 2002b, p. 87). Instead of individual "parts," wholes may consist of smaller entities, at different scales, each with their own localised quality of wholeness. Such sub-wholes are denoted as "living centres," which can be described as interrelated focal points within the larger whole, each reflecting "an organized zone of space, which because of its internal coherence, and because of its relation to its context, *exhibits centeredness*" (Alexander 2002b, p. 84).

The value of the concept of living centers is that it captures the main features that make a difference for our experience of the world, and contributes to its wholeness. In terms of design it thereby becomes a possible means of navigating the challenge of achieving wholeness by providing cues about focal points within it. What is important to notice here, however, is that following the holistic mindset, the centers that make up a given wholeness do not exist independently, but only become centers as a result of the configuration of the whole. Hence, one cannot simply "break down" an overall design challenge into design of individual centers, but have to maintain a simultaneous focus on the whole as well as the parts.

Alexander's perspective on good design as "living" wholes of form and context has some profound implications for the *process* of design. In terms of process, Alexander emphasizes that new design with the quality of wholeness or life never just appears out of nowhere but always *evolves* from a previous state of wholeness, initial qualities of which it is able to maintain or expand. Methodologically, this is reflected in the principle of "structure-preserving" (Alexander 2002b) or "wholeness-extending" transformations (Alexander 2007), through which living form-context ensembles gradually evolve, or "unfold," over time (Figure 5.1). The unfolding of wholes through wholeness-extending transformations builds on the fundamental view of Alexander's that *future* design wholeness is already *latently present* in current wholeness, and that designing therefore has to be a process of step-by-step adaptation of form and context toward increasing quality and complexity, rather than a matter of defining a desired end-state up front, and then setting out to produce this efficiently and with little or no change. Wholeness and life is, according to Alexander, simply not something that can just be defined or specified and then built. Like generated structures in nature it inherently has to emerge from a growth process of modification and adaptation that happens gradually in response to feedback about "the extent to which an emerging structure supports and embellishes the whole" (Alexander 2002b, p. 230). Or as more pragmatically expressed by Moggridge (2007), in design "whatever you come up with will automatically build on the past," and hence "if you are designing a new version of something that already exists, "state-of-the-art" is the most useful starting point" (Moggridge 2007, p. 728).

Figure 5.1: Six wholeness-extending transformations (left to right) (Alexander 2002b, p. 52).

While Alexander provides lengthy and detailed discussions about the properties of holistic and living processes and incites a process "*which can support the continuous creation of an emerging living structure in the world*" (Alexander 2002b, p. 508), he does not himself present a straightforward operational model or methodology of what such process may look like in practice. Hence, the question remains about how exactly we may procedurally go about achieving wholeness in design?

Overall, Alexander states that the types of processes that are capable of intensifying wholeness are the ones that place more emphasis on the context, and, in doing so, encourage the use of wholeness-extending transformations, and the creation of living centers. He also states that such processes must be "morphogenetic," or "architectural," meaning that they *create coherent form in the world* and explicitly emphasize this form-creating aspect of the process—that is its "designerly" nature, to use Cross's (1982) term. Thirdly, he highlights that in order to create unpredictable (i.e., non-trivial) or unexpected outcomes (Nelson and Stolterman 2003), the design process must be open-ended and itself partly unpredictable in order to truly accommodate for unforeseen adaptation and unfoldings of form and context. According to Alexander, such open-ended, unpredictable, morphogenetic processes, may only be achieved through step-by-step adaptation with appropriate feedback mechanisms for continually assessing the outcome of the process so far, and informing its immediate future direction. "*The process must go gradually, in a way that allows assessments, corrections, and improvements to be made about the degree of life which occurs throughout the structure, at all scales and at all levels. This process must occur continually throughout the conception, design and construction*" (Alexander 2002b, p. 237). Hence, the designer needs to be able to shift focus and technique as *needed* whenever in the process—go back to the drawing board, study an aspect of context more in depth, build and test a prototype, analyze data from a new perspective—instead of being confined to a predefined sequence of activities. A process like this is inherently contextual, iterative and multidirectional. It views the world as inseparable from its history, current context, and threads into the future. It unfolds stepwise but can at any point go in any direction, and it has no predefined starting or ending points.

CHAPTER 6

Revisiting User-Centered Design

In light of these perspectives on design, I will now turn my attention back to the prevailing user-centered design (UCD) approach to interaction design, and respond to some of the shortcomings of this approach discussed in contemporary interaction design research.

As described earlier, user-centered design typically follows a cycle consisting of four stages in which we study, design, build, and evaluate technology, as depicted in Figure 6.1. Other labels exist, but essentially they denote the same activities (Harper et al. 2008).

Figure 6.1: The traditional, four-stage UCD model (based on Harper et al. 2008).

One of the shortcomings of the UCD model, which I often hear from students and practitioners, is that it is almost too simplistic and high level. It does not say much about the outcomes from each stage, what they are, and how they differ. It is also unclear how the iterative nature of the model actually works: how different iterations can take different shapes and have different outcomes, and how continuous iteration is cumulative and going forwards toward better outcomes, rather than just going around in a circle. Looking at support for how to iterate through the stages it is also unclear why the activity of "evaluating" is followed by the activity of "studying." If working iteratively by designing on the basis of user studies, and then evaluating prototypes by putting these back in the hands of prospective users, then aren't evaluating and studying in fact two variations of the same type of empirical activity? Finally, it can be questioned if a predefined linear sequence really depicts the quintessence of well-functioning interaction design processes, or if such processes are in fact, or ought to be, far more elastic and irregular?

That said there are, of course, examples of researchers and practitioners who in practice already take a less linear approach to UCD as, for example, described by Moggridge (2007). However, when and how to "deviate" from the overall UCD process model is not well described in the literature, and doing so is therefore mostly based on people's individual experience with research and design in practice, and very difficult to learn to do well. For the design of mobile interactions in a continually unfolding manner, as described by Alexander (2002b), being limited to the potential linearity of the UCD model is particularly problematic exactly because it does not explicitly support the need to shift focus and technique as needed in light of the product as it onfolds.

In response to some of the shortcomings of the traditional UCD process model, the recent Microsoft research report "Being Human: Human-Computer Interaction in the Year 2020" (Harper et al. 2008) proposed that the traditional four-stage UCD model is extended with an additional stage in order to better accommodate for "third wave" (Bødker 2006) HCI research that focuses on human values and shaping society's new relationships with emerging ecosystems of computer technologies (Figure 6.2). The additional stage is labelled "understand" and is placed into the model as an initial activity of conceptual analysis to "focus on human values and to pinpoint those that we wish to design for and to research" (Harper et al. 2008, p. 59). It is a stage meant to involve specifying what kinds of people are the focus of a particular project, and understanding their domains of activity, cultures etc. which will in turn "either point to some fundamental research which needs to be carried out in Stage 2, or will provide guidance toward relevant research which has already been carried out" (Harper et al. 2008, p. 59). While it is noted that understanding a problem is traditionally a part of studying, it is proposed that "it be elevated to become a more explicit process, where the various human values at play are thought through and the trade-offs are examined in a systematic way" (Harper et al. 2008, p. 58).

Figure 6.2: The extended, five-stage UCD model (based on Harper et al. 2008).

The motivation behind this extended approach to HCI research and design is sound. In the third wave of HCI research, understanding the contextual richness and width of the people, activities, cultures, etc., that we are designing for is hugely important. However, I find myself unconvinced by the wedging-in of this "understanding" stage.

One of the problems, as I see it, is that it further sub-divides the already overlapping activities of evaluating and studying with a stage that essentially doesn't fit there. How can you really understand something before you study it? Another problem is that the proposed new stage to "understand" does not really type-match the other four stages in the model. Studying, designing, building and evaluating are to me all *activities*—something you can say to be doing. Understanding is not. It is the *outcome* or *purpose* of an activity. Thereby the proposed extended model in my view confuses the "how" and the "what" of the process of interaction design. While it might make perfect sense to suggest that the first stage of a design or research project should be to "understand" something, the question that needs to be raised in order to inform the creation or refinement of a better process model must necessarily be *how* this understanding is obtained? My suggested answer to this is simple: *study* and *analyze*. If we wish to understand the broader contexts of an interaction design challenge better, which I agree we should, then it is a matter of specifying more explicitly *what* should be studied and analyzed, in that particular iteration of the process, and *how* it should be done in order to generate the desired insight.

In response to this, and informed by the discussion of design research, I suggest considering three alternative changes to the traditional UCD approach:

1. separating and redefining activities and outcomes;

2. shifting the gravity point away from user-centeredness; and

3. making the process flexible and unpredictable.

6.1   SEPARATING AND REDEFINING ACTIVITIES AND OUTCOMES

My first suggestion for change is about activities and outcomes. In the alternative modification of the traditional UCD model depicted in Figure 6.3, three key factors are changed. First, the activities and the outcomes are separated. Activities are depicted as arrows in a circle while the outcomes are depicted outside the circle toward the top or bottom. This explicitly highlights the dual-purpose of interaction design research and practice: it is about creating *understanding* and *artifacts*. Understanding is the result of the activities of studying and analyzing, and artifacts (i.e., interactive systems) are the result of the activities of designing and building. Where understanding constitutes the foundation on which artifacts are designed and built, conversely artifacts, whether they are the designer's prototypes or already existing ones in the use context, constitute the foundation on which understanding is created through studying and analyzing. Second, the activities of evaluating and studying have been merged into one, reflecting the view that evaluating is, in fact, a *type* of studying and that differentiating between the two creates an unclear intersection between them from the point of view of the overall iterative process. Third, the activity of *analyzing* has been added as an explicit stage between studying and designing. This reflects the view that we do indeed need to elevate the importance of developing theoretical and conceptual understanding of the problem at hand in all of its richness and detail, including issues such as human values, context of use, and user experience. However, this is reconceptualised here as an explicit activity of *analysis* closely related, *but subsequent*, to the activity of studying. This activity *leads* to understanding.

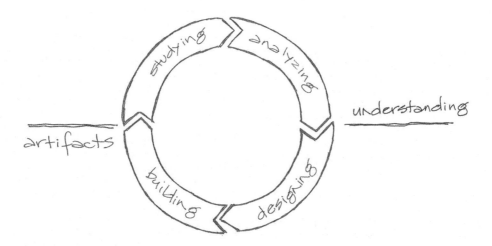

Figure 6.3: Revised and extended four-stage UCD model. Understanding and artifacts represent the two primary types of outcomes produced during the top and bottom two activities.

6.2 SHIFTING THE GRAVITY POINT

My second suggestion for change is about focus. In response to the ongoing debate about UCD being inadequate for informing the creation of novel and innovative interactive systems due to its built-in orbit around *users*, my second suggestion is to change this fundamental point of gravity toward one that better captures the essence of the emergent challenges at hand. In his 2005 Interactions magazine column, "Human-Centered Design Considered Harmful," Donald Norman (2005) already alluded to such fundamental change in gravity point by proposing *Activity*-Centered Design (ACD) as an alternative to UCD. Activity-centered design doesn't focus on user goals or preferences but instead more broadly on what they are doing (Saffer 2007). Although this suggestion is a step in the right direction, making "activity" the centre of orbit still doesn't quite suffice—at least not in the case of *mobile* interaction design. In order to better fit the challenges of designing mobile interactions, the gravity point, or unit of analysis, really needs to be shifted toward one with a wide enough scope to encompass the more extensive phenomena of *contextual user experiences* in a holistic way. Activity is a part of this, but equally so are other factors such as settings, people, artifacts, technologies, time, and more importantly the contextual whole that is made up by all of these. A similar point of view is made by Bill Moggridge (2007) in a critical self-reflection on the scope of the people centered prototyping approach used at IDEO, when he asks: "Is this focus on people and prototypes enough? Can we rely on just those two simple strategies to create excellent designs? I'm afraid not, as the constraints will come from the *full context* of the design problem, not just the people. (Moggridge 2007, p. 725, italics added). He continues, "you will need to understand as much as possible about everything that will affect the solution (…) find out as much as [you] can about the *context*" (Moggridge 2007, p. 726, italics added). In response to this, and echoing Alexander's (2002–2005) views on design as a continual interplay between form and context discussed earlier, I suggest that a better point of gravity for mobile interaction design would be *the ensemble, symbiosis, or convergence of form and context*. This is illustrated in Figure 6.4.

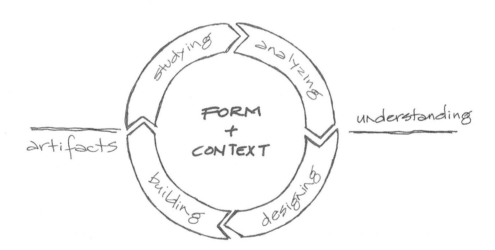

Figure 6.4: Shifting the gravity point to form-context syntheses rather than users.

Shifting the gravity point of the underlying process model from users to form-context convergence echoes the need for emerging interdisciplinary research fields to change the unit of analysis toward one that transcends the individual contributing disciplines as discussed previously. Using this conceptual optic on the revised approach in Figure 6.5, the activities of studying, analyzing, designing, and building are all about considering the ensemble of a particular form (an interactive mobile system) in relation to its context (users, technology, settings, activities, etc.) from different perspectives, with the purpose of producing either understanding or artifacts depending on whether you are in the top or the bottom part of the circle. Consequently, the interaction design process becomes neither user- nor technology-centered but instead transcends and continuously includes both of these viewpoints within a broader perspective on the contextual whole in which users and technologies interact.

Putting form-context convergence in the centre also respond to the concerns raised by, among others, Rasmussen (2007) that the original intentions of human-centeredness, as envisioned in the 1970's, have in UCD degenerated to being a limited paradigm of creating user friendly computer interfaces rather than focusing on the broader societal issues facing human kind through "socially useful production" and "human machine symbiosis." While some of the thoughts behind human-centeredness can still be still traced in the user-centered design literature, the focus has become predominantly on how people interact with computers rather than on "how the technology can be shaped to support enrichment of human skills and socially useful products" (Rasmussen 2007, p. 475). According to Gasson (2003) and Rasmussen (2007), a similar tendency can also be observed within the discipline of Interaction Design when the discourse starts with the concept of computer-based technology and when designers "ignore the context of design as systems situated in physically and socially constituted environments" (Rasmussen 2007, p. 476). Rather than producing socially and holistically useful products, this results in incremental or "problem-closure" development of products framed by relatively limited tasks in isolation from the social world that surrounds them (Gasson 2003, p. 36). In reaction to this, Rasmussen (2007) proposes a "human-context centered" approach revitalising the original intentions of the human-centered tradition and promoting the fundamental view that "although human beings are important creatures in the world, they are still a part of a much larger context of natural and social relationships, in which they should try to act and interact in a sustainable manner" (Rasmussen 2007, p. 478). At the core of this proposal is the principle of dialectical thinking in order to overcome the weaknesses of differentiating between technology- and user-centered approaches. Rather than making such clean-cut distinction, or finding an optimal balance between the two, a possible *fusion* of the opposing interests and forces is sought by transcending to the higher-level unity of form-context convergence.

6.3   MAKING THE PROCESS FLEXIBLE AND UNPREDICTABLE

My third suggestion for change is about process. In light of the view that designerly processes of creation unfold stepwise through unpredictable sequences of assessment, corrections and improvements of form-context ensembles with respect to their larger whole, my third suggestion is to discard the view that interaction design should follow a predefined cyclical sequence of activities, like the one depicted in the traditional UCD model. Inspired by Alexander (2002–2005), I instead propose a web process model that explicitly allows unpredictable, less orderly, and more complex sequences of design, allowing the designer to shift focus and techniques as deemed necessary on basis of the continual consideration of outcomes so far. This is illustrated in Figure 6.5.

The key difference between this and the traditional cyclical UCD approach is that it encourages a much more flexible and pragmatic way of dealing with the design challenge at hand. Rather than being stuck in a particular activity until it is "finished," and then having to wait for a whole iteration before attending to this activity again, a web, or "stepping stone" (Stokholm 2008, 2010), approach allows the designer to jump freely and frequently between activities, thereby responding better to the emergent needs of the process, and letting the evolving form-context symbiosis control the process rather than the other way around. Clockwise circular sequences are of course not prevented, but they only happen when considered appropriate.

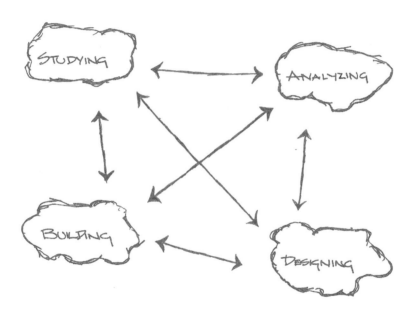

Figure 6.5: Replacing the predefined cyclical sequence of activities with a flexible web process model that allows unpredictable, less orderly, and more complex sequences.

By taking a more flexible and unpredictable process like the one depicted in Figure 6.5 as the methodological foundation for design, rather than a predefined cyclic one as prescribed by UCD, one would in fact support what often happens in real-world interaction design practice, as described by Bill Moggridge (2007, pp. 649-650, pp. 729-730). One would recognize that the most successful design processes are usually out of sequence, apparently unstructured, and sometimes almost seem random—like the ball bouncing in unexpected directions inside a pinball machine, to use Moggridge's own analogy—and acknowledge the knowledge among experienced designers, that the fastest way to achieve a successful design is to use the tools and techniques of the trade "quickly and repeated frequently, but usually not in the same order" (Moggridge 2007, p. 729).

CHAPTER 7

Continual Convergence of Form and Context

With the designerly ways of thinking and working in mind, and in response to the prevailing user-centered approach discussed, what then could an alternative, designerly, and contextually oriented, approach to designing mobile interactions then look like?

As we move toward a society of increasingly widespread pervasive computing and digital ecologies, the design of mobile interactions accordingly needs to transcend existing approaches and develop a holistic and contextual view on technology design. My approach to doing this is to use the ensemble of form and context as our central unit of analysis and embrace a designerly way of achieving convergence between form and context through a contextually grounded, wholeness sensitive, and continually unfolding process of design. I describe such an approach to designing mobile interactions as one of *continual convergence of form and context*. This approach describes the dual-purpose unfolding of mobile interaction design research and practice, and ties together empirical, creative, technical and theoretical types of work and thinking that takes place within the design activities of studying, analyzing, designing, and building interactive mobile systems and user experiences. It is neither user- nor technology-centered, but instead encourages truly interdisciplinary research and design at the intersection between technology and liberal arts by transcending these two viewpoints.

This approach to designing mobile interactions can be characterized and described by the following seven principles:

1. emergence and unpredictability;

2. form and context unity;

3. form and context convergence;

4. oscillation between understanding and artifacts;

5. oscillation between concrete and abstract;

6. four types of design activity; and

7. four types of design ripples.

These principles are illustrated and described in the following.

7.1   EMERGENCE AND UNPREDICTABILITY

In designing mobile interactions the emergence of new artifacts and understanding happens by continually stepping between the four activities of studying, analyzing, designing, and building. The sequence of activities is not predefined cyclical but flexible and multidirectional, meaning that the designer can jump freely and frequently between activities as needed in response to the continual consideration of outcomes and emergent needs, challenges and opportunities. This allows the process of form-context convergence to be stepwise but unpredictable (Alexander 2002–2005) and less orderly (Moggridge 2007), yet continual and cumulative. This is depicted in Figure 7.1 where the upward spiral illustrates the cumulative convergence of form and context as the design process unfolds.

Departing further from the circular UCD models, this approach emphasizes the evolving character of iterative research and design where each step through a particular activity is purposely different from the last time in terms of focus, scope and type of outcome. For example, the empirical activity of "studying" is different depending on whether it is an early activity of inquiring into the context of a design challenge, or if it is a later activity of inquiring into the user experience of a new interactive prototype system. Similarly, theoretical research involves different levels of analytical abstraction depending on how many steps we have been through, and leads to increasingly higher levels of understanding from each oscillation between the concrete and the abstract. As the process unfolds over time, designs are increasingly detailed and refined, and the design artifacts we produce are created with increasing levels of fidelity and completeness.

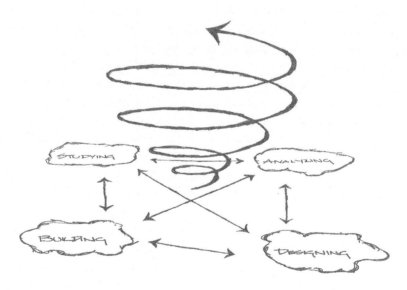

Figure 7.1: An unpredictable and continual process toward convergence of form and context.

This view on the interaction design process obviously takes some of its inspiration from Boehm's (1988) spiral model for systems development iterating through particular phases, emphasising that each iteration is different from, and builds on, the previous one. But it is different from Boehm's model in the sense that it does not to the same degree dictate a spiralling sequence of specific activities in detail, and that it traces the processes through very different types of stages. Also, whereas Boehm's model is a tool for managing a software development process through careful planning and risk management, the continually cumulative aspect of designing mobile interactions serves the purpose of illustrating that each step of studying, analyzing, designing, and building creates additional empirical, theoretical, creative, and technical insight and value in relation to the design that unfolds from the process.

7.2 FORM AND CONTEXT UNITY

The basic unit of analysis in my view on the design of mobile interactions is the unity of form and context. Putting the unity of form and context in the centre echoes the contextual view that the world is inherently dynamic, that the relationship between context and form is a continually changing one, and that design is therefore about the construction of both of these in concert. This view essentially transcends user- and technology-centeredness. This is illustrated in Figure 7.2 where form and context are depicted as an intertwined unity, creating a whole that is bigger than the sum of its individual parts.

Figure 7.2: Form and context as an intertwined unity.

In the design of mobile interactions the unity of form and context provides a common reference point for the activities of studying, analyzing, designing and building. Echoing the early work of Alexander (1964), "form" does not just mean shape, but is the unity of *shape, look, function,* and *content*—i.e., the interactive system artifacts we design. Context is what defines or frames the situation in which these interactive systems or forms are deployed. Elaborating on Alexander's work, the design of mobile interactions is about actively designing not only the form but also the context—i.e., designing new use situations and practices.

7.3   FORM AND CONTEXT CONVERGENCE

The unpredictable and continual process and the unity of form and context is tied together in Figure 7.3 below. In this view on the design of mobile interactions, the unity of form and context is continually explored and refined by stepping between the four activities of *studying, analyzing, designing,* and *building* in an unpredictable order gradually leading to the emergence of new artifacts and understanding. Throughout this process, the designer can step from any of the four corners to any of the others, meaning that the sequence of activities is not fixed but flexible. The result of the process is the gradual and unpredictable emergence of form-context convergence.

Each of the four activities contribute to the unfolding of design and gradual convergence of form and context through "ripples" of *assessment, abstraction, exploration,* and *synthesis* toward the specific ensemble of form and context in the centre. In stepping freely between activities, the interaction design process oscillates between producing *understanding* and *artifacts*, and between working with the *concrete* and with the *abstract*.

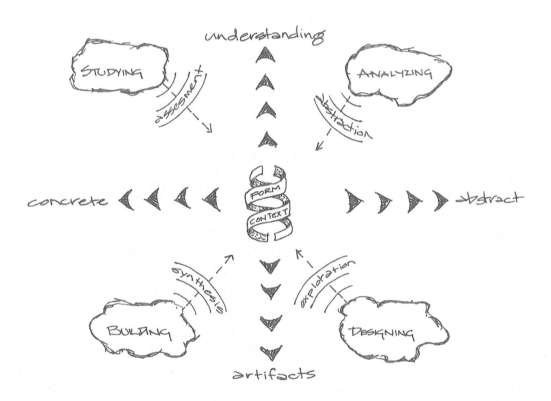

Figure 7.3: Form and context convergence.

The proposed model above encourages a more flexible and pragmatic way of designing mobile interactions, while at the same time defining a shared focus for all activities and describing how they each contribute to the unfolding of the whole.

7.4   BETWEEN UNDERSTANDING AND ARTIFACTS

The distinction between producing understanding and artifacts reflects the contextual view that design is a matter of constructing both problem-understandings and solution-propositions through a cyclical process of learning about a situation, and responding to it through suggestions for design. This is illustrated in Figure 7.4 depicting a design process with oscillations of changing frequencies and amplitude, reflecting the continual and unpredictable sequence of activities, and a tendency toward increasingly mature understanding and artifacts.

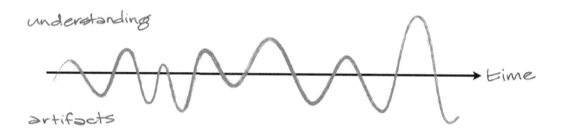

Figure 7.4: Oscillating between producing understanding and artifacts.

In designing mobile interactions, understanding results from the activities of studying and analyzing, and artifacts results from designing and building. Understanding is the foundation on which artifacts are designed and built, and artifacts are vehicles for creating understanding through study and analysis. In the design of mobile interactions, artifacts cover the range of tangible design products emerging from the process such as sketches, models, mock-ups, simulations, prototypes, and functional systems. On the opposite side, understanding covers the range of less tangible products from the process such as empirical data, personas, scenarios, models, concepts, frameworks, and theory.

7.5   BETWEEN CONCRETE AND ABSTRACT

Introducing a distinction into the form and context convergence model between working with the concrete and working with the abstract is inspired by related discussions of the process of interleaved research and design by, for example, Dubberly et al. (2008), IDEO (2009), Mendel and Yeager (2010), and Dubberly and Evenson (2011). In these discussions it is suggested that the two major phases of a design process of analysis and synthesis (respectively, leading to understanding and to artifacts) both involve an orthogonal continuum between "the concrete work we inhabit or could inhabit" and "abstractions and models of what is or what could be, which we imagine and share with others" (Dubberly et al. 2008). It is by elevating our understanding from a concrete to an abstract level before attempting to move from understanding toward new form (i.e., interactive systems), and by exploring new form opportunities in the abstract before implementing and assessing interactive system artifacts in the concrete, that we are able to talk about a process as one of *design* as opposed to one of simple, or *unselfconscious* (Alexander 1964), form making. Bridging between understanding and artifacts on an abstract rather than a concrete level is also what facilitates the conception of solutions beyond incremental improvements to misfit through unreflective reaction. During the design process we continually shift between these two ends of the orthogonal continuum. This is depicted in Figure 7.5, illustrating the same pattern of oscillations with changing frequencies and amplitude caused by the unpredictable sequence of activities.

Figure 7.5: Oscillating between working with the abstract and the concrete.

In designing mobile interactions, empirical and technical research takes place in the concrete end of the continuum, dealing with studying and building "what is" and "what could be." In the other end of the continuum, theoretical and creative research takes place in the abstract, analyzing and designing what is and what could be. Introducing the concrete-abstract continuum into the model emphasizes important differences between studying/analyzing and designing/building, and guides the transition between these activities toward ones of *abstraction* and *synthesis*, as discussed more further below.

7.6   FOUR TYPES OF DESIGN ACTIVITY

The two orthogonal distinctions between creating understanding or artifacts and between working with the concrete or the abstract define a space involving four distinct types of work: empirical, theoretical, creative, and technical, and illustrate that the design of mobile interactions involves all of these. This is outlined in Table 7.1.

Table 7.1: Four types of design activity		
	Concrete	**Abstract**
Understanding	**Empirical** Studying: working with practice	**Theoretical** Analyzing: working with concepts
Artifacts	**Technical** Building: working with prototypes	**Creative** Designing: working with opportunities

In the top left quadrant, mobile interaction design is *empirical*. Empirical work embraces the fundamental concept of modern science that insight must be based on observable evidence—or empirical data. When designing mobile interactions, being in the empirical quadrant means that we are working with the practice or actuality in which our products and solutions are supposed to fit and be used. This work is done through studies of real-world practice using empirical methods such as observations, probes and experimentation, and covers the empirical study of people, technology, and context.

In the top right quadrant, mobile interaction design is *theoretical*. Theoretical work seeks to explain empirical phenomena in a consistent way, enabling us to understand and predict a given subject matter. When designing mobile interactions, being in the theoretical quadrant means that we are working with theoretical models and descriptions of our subject matter. This is done through analyzing empirical data using theoretical frameworks and concepts derived either from previous research or produced through grounded theory or analysis.

Moving to the bottom right quadrant, mobile interaction design becomes *creative*. Creative work is a process by which a person creates something novel that is of value for other people, society, etc. When designing mobile interactions, being in the creative quadrant means that we are working with new opportunities for mobile computing inspired and informed by our empirical and theoretical insight and our knowledge about the potentials of technology. This is done by conceiving and refining original design ideas and solutions through an iterative process of designing potential artifacts and products making use of flexible and incomplete design instantiations such as sketches, models, and mock-ups, that are purposely suggestive, explorative, and even provocative, rather than descriptive, delimited, and definitive.

Finally, in the bottom left quadrant, mobile interaction design is *technical*. Technical work in this relation seeks to provide concrete instantiations of design propositions or solutions in response to opportunities, problems, challenges or needs. When designing mobile interactions, being in the technical quadrant means that we are working with prototypes of our proposed design ideas. This is done through the building of artifacts such as simulations, prototypes, or functional systems, investigating technical feasibility, and subsequently enabling empirical investigations of use quality.

7.7   FOUR TYPES OF DESIGN RIPPLES

The distinction between four types of interaction design work naturally leads on to four types of design ripples emerging from these. These ripples, or pulses, describe what happens in the oscillations between the concrete and the abstract, and between artifacts and understanding. In designing mobile interactions they can be described as pulses of abstraction, exploration, synthesis, and assessment, happening, respectively, when analyzing, designing, building, and studying (Figure 7.6).

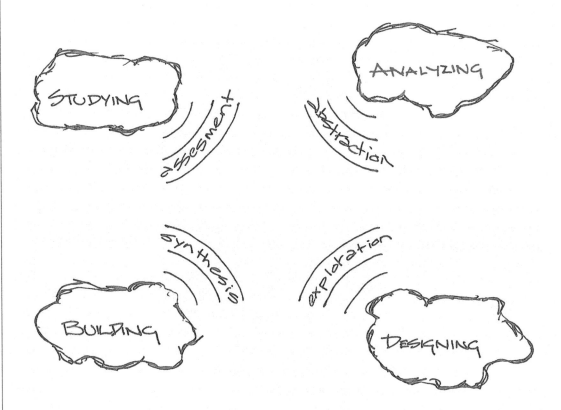

Figure 7.6: Ripples in the design of mobile interactions.

Abstraction happens when progressing toward abstract theoretical frameworks and concepts from, for example, concrete empirical data. It is about learning more from the world around us. In designing mobile interactions the purpose of this transition is to elevate the level of understanding about context beyond concrete observations and descriptive accounts, and distill insights that explain the observed phenomena. This is done by analyzing our data, filtering it, prioritizing it, and organizing it, and in doing so moving further and further away from the concrete, and from artifacts.

Exploration happens when moving either from analysis or building to design. While going back to the drawing board informed by experiences with a prototype system is not particularly difficult, bridging the gap between understanding and artifacts is often perceived as the hard bit of the design process. This is because rather than elaborating on a previous stage with the same type of aim, it is an orthogonal direction of work with a completely different type of outcome. As described by Dubberly et al. (2008), this transition is what lies "at the heart of designing"—moving from analysis to design, from problem to solution, from the current situation to the future, from research toward prototypes. It is about opening up a design space for future form. In designing mobile interactions the purpose of this transition is to use our understanding of context as foundation for investigating and suggesting what the future might look like, or to change our design in light of new technical insight. This is done by speculating, hypothesizing, and imagining possible futures in abstract form, and grounded in data and theory.

Synthesis happens when progressing toward concrete prototypes from, for example, abstract design. It is the opposite transition to abstraction and is about making things real. In designing mobile interactions the purpose of this transition is to manifest our design ideas in concrete artifacts showcasing what the future could actually look like and making it available for us in a tangible form that can be put into context. This is done by synthesizing design ideas and technologies into concrete interactive systems, and bringing them to life through prototype implementations investigating the feasibility of our ideas and concepts. In doing so we move further and further away from the abstract.

Assessment happens when moving either from building or analyzing to studying. This is the opposite transition to exploration and is about measuring the quality of our design instantiations or examining our theoretical understanding in order to improve them. Like exploration, assessment may involve an orthogonal direction of work from abstraction and synthesis, and crossing a gap that is hard to bridge. Crossing back from artifacts to understanding is difficult and sometimes overlooked as an important and integrated part of the design process. Instead, "evaluation" is often left as an appendix, and the subsequent process sadly shortcut by heading unreflected into re-implementation rather than seeking better understanding in order to subsequently explore radically different design opportunities. In designing mobile interactions the purpose of this transition is to return to the empirical realm of work that laid the grounds for our understanding and artifacts in the first place. This is done by feeding our theories or designs back into their context of origin, or intended context of use, assessing their fitness, and using our newly gained insight as the starting point for further abstraction, exploration, or synthesis.

Together these four ripples capture the basic elements of an interaction design process.

CHAPTER 8

Where to from Here?

In the preceding chapters I presented a contextual approach to designing contemporary interactive mobile computer systems that promotes a designerly way of achieving convergence between form and context through a wholeness sensitive and continually unfolding process of design. In the following, I will summarize the thinking presented and discussed as three main points of observation. I will then put forward some thoughts about potential challenges and limitations of a contextual approach, and, finally, some thoughts about where we can go from here.

8.1 THREE MAIN POINTS

In brief, the thinking presented and discussed throughout this book can be summarized in the three main points below.

1	**Transcending Technology- and User-Centeredness** Mobile interaction design has become a discipline at the intersection between technology and liberal arts where the best results yield from combining the two. Doing this well requires approaches that transcend technology- and user-centeredness.
2	**Form-Context Unity** Form-context unity is a central concept in all phases of designing mobile interactions. This makes it a suitable higher-level unit of analysis for interdisciplinary research and design transcending focus beyond technology- or user-centeredness.
3	**A Designerly Way** Contextual interaction design guides the continual convergence of form and context through a process of shifting freely between empirical, theoretical, creative, and technical work, oscillating between artifacts and understanding, concrete and abstract.

8.1.1 TRANSCENDING TECHNOLOGY- AND USER-CENTEREDNESS

Mobile interaction design has become a discipline at the intersection between technology and liberal arts where the best results yield from combining the two. Doing this well requires approaches that transcend technology- and user-centeredness. Although current mobile interaction design is multi-methodological and involves multiple disciplines, there is still an assumption that users and technology can advantageously be studied separately. In contrast, taking a contextual approach to interaction design means that focus is explicitly broadened to the higher-level unity of form and context. Combining and integrating methods and techniques from different disciplines into new and hybrid ones, with a transcendent unit of analysis, allows us to maintain this broader focus throughout all of the different activities of the interaction design process.

8.1.2   FORM-CONTEXT UNITY

Form-context unity is a central concept in all phases of designing mobile interactions. This makes it a suitable higher-level unit of analysis for interdisciplinary research and design transcending focus beyond technology- or user-centeredness. Viewing the design of mobile interactions as continual convergence of form and context facilitates a paradigmatic shift stimulating new ways of conceptualizing and working by framing new issues, research questions and challenges beyond those of the disciplines involved with mobile interaction design individually. As a central unit of analysis, form-context unity provides a wide enough scope to encompass the more extensive phenomena of mobile interaction design user experience in a holistic way. From a contextual perspective the activities of studying, analyzing, designing, and building are all about considering the ensemble of a particular form in relation to its context: an interactive mobile system in relation to users, technology, settings, activities, etc. Consequently, the interaction design process becomes neither user- nor technology-centered but instead continuously includes both of these viewpoints within a broader perspective.

8.1.3   A DESIGNERLY WAY

Contextual approaches to interaction design guides the continual convergence of form and context through an unpredictable process of shifting freely between empirical, theoretical, creative, and technical work, oscillating between producing artifacts and understanding, and between working in the concrete and in the abstract. The process of stepping freely between the activities of studying, analyzing, designing and building creates what can be described as ripples of abstraction, exploration, synthesis, and assessment toward the unity of form and context, which is always in focus and continually evolving. In this way, viewing the design of mobile interactions as continual convergence of form and context promotes a designerly way of thinking and working where new knowledge, artifacts, and contexts emerge from a series of intentionally short and open ended steps. It allows us to do mobile interaction design that is intentionally rhetorical, exploratory, emergent, opportunistic, abductive, reflective, ambiguous, and risky, and it allows us to reach beyond interaction design as a matter of problem setting and solving, and treat it also as a matter of creating entirely new practices—enabling humans to do things in their lives that they couldn't do before.

8.2   CHALLENGES FOR A CONTEXTUAL APPROACH

Reaching the end of this book, some questions still need to be addressed further. What are, for example, the potential challenges and limitations of such contextual approach and holistic view? And where do we go from here?

One potential challenge for taking a contextual approach to interaction design process rather than a traditional user- or technology-centered one is that the concept of *context*, and *form-context ensembles*, may appear too abstract and difficult to grasp. In contrast, *users* are entities that we can relatively easy define, identify, study, and simply go and talk to if we don't quite understand them. Similarly, *technology* is a relatively tangible thing in interaction design that we can often simply look at, touch, and try out. The intangibility of entities like context and wholeness make them more difficult to deal with by comparison. If a contextual approach to interaction design is to succeed, we will need to explore it further, and to develop concepts, techniques, and best practices that makes it accessible for interaction designers and interaction deign researchers to embrace and practice contextual and holistic thinking in their work. My own contributions to this included in this boo are steps in that direction. But they are in no capacity complete. My hope is that this is something others will find interesting to pursue, and that researchers and practitioners currently grounded in user- or technology-centered design will not see the views that I have presented here as a strike against the quality or importance of their work. After all, taking a contextual approach is not a matter of throwing away the legacy of user- or technology-centered design at all. It is a matter of trying to include both of these viewpoints, equally, and within a broader scope that enables us to transcend them.

8.3   DOWNSIDES OF HOLISM IN INTERACTION DESIGN

In terms of the downsides of a holistic view on interaction design, an obvious concern is that by focusing on the whole, you might erroneously neglect or ignore important details of the parts. This is a valid concern, and one that is important to keep clear in mind when taking a holistic stance. The kind of holistic thinking that I have promoted in this book falls within what Edmonds (1999) calls *pragmatic holism*. Rather than the all-embracing view of a system in *experiential* holism, this is the kind of *nonlinear* holism that refers to the phenomenon of emergence in that "when A and B are combined, the resulting C has more properties than what each of the components bring" (Raman 2005). While reductionism may struggle to deal with such phenomena of emergence in complex systems and how individual elements can converge into something very different, holism on the other hand may struggle to deal with identifying and explaining what "lies beneath" a larger whole in a way that enables us to understand it, and possibly reproduce it.

Essentially, these concerns put us in the middle of the highly polarised debate about whether reductionism or holism is the better approach for viewing and dealing with the world (see, for example, Edmonds 1999, Raman 2005). I won't go into this debate here, but to say that in my opinion neither of the two are, in their extreme forms, very useful positions to hold as interaction designers or interaction design researchers. What is needed in interaction design are world views that are less dogmatic and more pragmatic, seeking useful accounts, models, and understandings of the phenomena in the world that we are interested in designing and designing for. Both reductionism and holism are legitimate and have value in this respect. But they provide us with very different pictures and understanding of the same phenomenon. As described by Raman (2005), like a microscope and a telescope, reductionism and holism are two powerful instruments to explore the world. "Each is relevant and important in its own context. The more we focus on one, the more the other becomes blurred. Thus, reductionism and holism are complementary in the Bohr sense of the term" (Raman 2005), and to get a full picture, we need them both. In the words of Herbert Simon "in the face of complexity, an in-principle reductionist may be at the same time a pragmatic holist" (Simon 1962). Conversely, an in-principle holist may at times need to apply reductionist principles when pragmatically useful and not compromising the overall view of the whole.

In mobile interaction design the reductionist view is already strongly present, but the complementary holistic view is not.

8.4   TOWARD DIGITAL ECOLOGY

The final thing I wish to touch upon is the notion of digital ecosystems and artifact ecologies. As discussed in Chapter 2, the currently emerging trend within mobile computing is the creation of digital ecosystems where interactive mobile systems and devices are viewed less in isolation and more as parts of larger use contexts or artifact ecologies (see, for example, Jung et al. 2008, Bødker and Klokmose 2011, O'Hara et al. 2011, Sørensen et al. 2014). In my opinion this is an avenue for further research that is particularly interesting, and one that I look forward to engaging myself in more deeply. As a starting point for this, I believe that the contextual approach on designing mobile interactions presented in this book holds potentials for designing digital ecosystems and artifact ecologies. The reason for this is that it already inolves designing for the whole and has a build-in sensitivity for the continual emergence and convergence of form and context that characterizes such ecosystems and ecologies. What is still needed, however, is the further development of a theoretical and conceptual lens through which we can view, address and describe this emerging phenomenon in a way that informs and inspires design and further thinking. This work may find inspiration and traction in some of the conceptually stronger and less technical literature on ubiquitous and pervasive computing that has started to appear in recent years, such as Adam Greenfield's book *Everyware* (2006).

As a way of encapsulating and labeling this work, I suggest using and developing the term *digital ecology*. Ecology is the study of elements making up an ecosystem, and is very generally about understanding the interactions between organisms and their environment. It is inherently holistic and has an interdisciplinary nature, and it is not synonymous with "the environment" or with "environmentalism." Nor is ecological thinking limited to the discipline of biology. For example, "industrial ecology" studies material and energy flows through networks of industrial processes, and "human ecology" is as interdisciplinary area of research that provides a framework for understanding and researching human social interaction. In a similar fashion, I believe "digital ecology" may be a useful way of describing the study of elements making up digital ecosystems and the holistic understanding of interactions between these elements and their environment. While the term "digital ecology" has elsewhere been used to describe the fusion of virtual end real life forms, or the mix of digital code and environmentalism, these are not related to my suggested use of the term. By digital ecology I simply refer to the study of interrelated digital systems (e.g., mobile and pervasive computing) and the processes by which these systems work and interact, and are conceived, emerge, converge, and evolve. It is about understanding the functioning, use, and experience of digital ecosystems and artifact ecologies around us, and the design processes that creates and advances them.

References

Abowd, G. D. and Mynatt E. D. (2000) Charting Past, Present and Future Research in Ubiquitous Computing. *ACM Transactions on Computer-Human Interaction*, 7(1), 29–58. DOI: 10.1145/344949.344988. 28, 30

Admob (2009) *March 2009 Metrics Report*. http://metrics.admob.com/. 14

Agre, P. (2001) Changing Places: Contexts of Awareness in Computing. *Human-Computer Interaction* 16(2), 177–192. DOI: 10.1207/S15327051HCI16234_04. 28, 29

Alexander, C. (2007) Empirical Findings from The Nature of Order. *Environmental & Architectural Phenomenology Newsletter*, winter 2007. 55, 56, 68

Alexander, C. (2005) The Nature of Order. *Vol. 3: A Vision of A Living World*. Berkeley, California: CES Publishing. 49, 51, 55, 63, 64, 68

Alexander, C. (2004) *The Nature of Order. Vol. 4: The Luminous Ground*. Berkeley, California: CES Publishing. 49, 51, 55, 63, 64, 68

Alexander, C. (2002b) *The Nature of Order. Vol. 2: The Process of Creating Life*. Berkeley, California: CES Publishing. 49, 51, 55, 56, 57, 60, 63, 64, 68

Alexander, C. (2002a) *The Nature of Order. Vol. 1: The Phenomenon of Life*. Berkeley, California: CES Publishing. 49, 51, 55, 63, 64, 68

Alexander, C. (1979) *The Timeless Way of Building*. New York: Oxford University Press. 49, 55

Alexander, C., Ishikawa, S., Silverstein, M. with Jacobson, M., Fiksdahl-King, I. and Angel, S. (1977) *A Pattern Language: Towns, Buildings, Constructions*. New York: Oxford University Press. 49, 55

Alexander, C. (1964) *Notes on the Synthesis of Form*. Cambridge, MA: Harvard University Press. 3, 48, 51, 55, 69, 72

Alvarez, I. and Kilbourn, B. (2002) Mapping the information society literature: topics, perspectives and root metaphors. *First Monday*, 7(1). DOI: 10.5210/fm.v7i1.922. 50

Aoki, P. M., Honicky, R. J., Mainwaring, A., Myers, C., Paulos, E., Subramanian, S., and Woodruff, A. (2009) A vehicle for research: using street sweepers to explore the landscape of environmental community action. In *Proceedings of CHI 2009*, Boston, MA (pp. 375–384). New York: ACM. DOI: 10.1145/1518701.1518762. 29

Archer, B. (1992) The nature of research in design and design education. In B. Archer, K. Baynes and P. Roberts (Eds.), *The Nature of Research into Design and Technology Education: Design Curriculum Matters*. Loughborough, UK: Loughborough University. 51, 52

Archer, B. (1965) *Systematic Method for Designers*. London: Council of Industrial Design. 48

Atkinson, P. (2005) Man in a Briefcase—The Social Construction of the Laptop Computer and the Emergence of a Type Form. *Journal of Design History*, 18(2), 191-205. DOI: 10.1093/jdh/epi024. 5, 7

Augsburg, T. (2005) *Becoming Interdisciplinary: An Introduction to Interdisciplinary Studies*. Kendall Hunt Publishing. 24

Bagnara, S. and Smith, G. S. (Eds.) (2006) *Theories and Practice in Interaction Design*. London: Lawrence Erlbaum Associates Publishers. 23

Ballard, B. (2007) *Designing the Mobile User Experience*. Padstow: John Wiley and Sons Ltd. DOI: 10.1002/9780470060575. 23

Bannon, L. (1992) Interdisciplinarity or interdisciplinary theory in CSCW? In *Workshop proceedings of CSCW 1992*. Workshop on Interdisciplinary Theory for CSCW Design, Toronto, Canada. 27

Bardram, J. E. (2009) Activity-based computing for medical work in hospitals. *ACM Transactions on Computer-Human Interaction*, 16(2), 1-36. DOI: 10.1145/1534903.1534907. 30

Barkhuus, L. and Dey, A. (2003) Is Context-Aware Computing Taking Control away from the User? Three Levels of Interactivity Examined. In *Proceedings of UbiComp 2003*, LNCS (pp. 149 – 156). Berlin: Springer-Verlag. DOI: 10.1007/978-3-540-39653-6_12.

Basili, V. R., Selby, R. W., and Hutchins, D. H. (1986) Experimentation in software engineering. *IEEE Transactions on Software Engineering, SE-12* (1986), 733-743. DOI: 10.1109/TSE.1986.6312975.

Benbasat, I. (1985) An analysis of research methodologies. In F. W. MacFarlan (Ed.) *The Information System Research Challenge* (pp. 47-85). Boston: Harvard Business School Press.

Benford S., Giannacji G., Koleva B., and Rodden T. (2009) From Interaction to Trajectories: Designing Coherent Journeys Through User Experiences. In *Proceedings of CHI 2009*, Boston, MA (pp. 709-718). New York: ACM. DOI: 10.1145/1518701.1518812. 30

Benyon, D., Turner, P., and Turner, S. (2005) *Designing Interactive Systems*. Harlow: Addison-Wesley. 23

Bergman E. (Ed.) (2000) *Information Appliances and Beyond*. San Francisco: Morgan Kaufmann Publishers

Bergman E. and Haitani R. (2000) Designing the PalmPilot: a Conversation with Rob Haitani. In E. Bergman (Ed.), *Information Appliances and Beyond*. San Francisco: Morgan Kaufmann Publishers. 8, 12, 13 23

Betiol, A. H. and de Abreu Cybis, W. (2005) Usability Testing of Mobile Devices: A Comparison of Three Approaches. In *Proceedings of INTERACT 2005*, LNCS (pp. 470-481). Berlin: Springer-Verlag. DOI: 10.1007/11555261_39. 30

Beyer, H. and Holtzblatt, K. (1998) *Contextual Design: Defining Customer-Centered Systems*. San Francisco: Morgan Kaufmann Publishers. DOI: 10.1145/291224.291229. 35

Blevis, E. and Stolterman, E. (2009) Transcending Disciplinary Boundaries in Interaction Design. *Interactions*, 16(5), 48-51. DOI: 10.1145/1572626.1572636. 25

Boehm, B. W. (1988) A Spiral Model of Software Development and Enhancement. *IEEE Computer*, 21(5), 61-72. DOI: 10.1109/2.59. 69

Bondo, J., Barnard, D., Burcaw, D., Novikoff, T., Kemper, C., Parrish, C., Peters, K., Siebert, J., and Wilson, E. (2009) *iPhone User Interface Design Projects*. Apress. 24

Bradley, N. A. and Dunlop, M. D. (2002) Understanding Contextual Interactions to Design Navigational Context-Aware Applications. In *Proceedings of Mobile HCI 2002* (pp. 349-353). Berlin: Springer Verlag. DOI: 10.1007/3-540-45756-9_37. 28, 30

Bratteteig, T. (2007) Design Research in Informatics: A response to Livari. *Scandinavian Journal of Information Systems*, 19(2), 65-75. 50

Brewster, S. (2002) Overcoming the Lack of Screen Space on Mobile Computers. *Personal and Ubiquitous Computing*, 6, 188-205. DOI: 10.1007/s007790200019. 30

Brolin, B. C. (1980) *Architecture in Context: Fitting New Buildings with Old*. New York: Van Nostrand Reinhold.54

Brown, B. and Randell, R. (2004) Building a Context-Sensitive Telephone: Some Hopes and Pitfalls for Context Sensitive Computing. *Computer-Supported Cooperative Work*, 13(3-4), 329-345. DOI: 10.1007/s10606-004-2806-4. 30

Brown, B. A., Sellen, A. J. ,and O'Hara, K. (2000) A diary study of information capture in working life. In *Proceedings of CHI 2000*, The Hague, The Netherlands (pp. 438-445). New York: ACM. DOI: 10.1145/332040.332472. 28

Buxton, B. (2007) *Sketching User Experiences: Getting the Design Right and the Right Design*. San Francisco: Morgan Kaufmann Publishers. 47

Buxton, W. (2001) Less is More (More or Less): Uncommon Sense and the Design of Computers. In P. Denning (Ed.), The *Invisible Future: The Seamless Integration of Technology in Everyday Life* (pp. 145-179). New York: McGraw Hill. 12

Bødker, S. and Klokmose, C. (2011) The Human-Artifact Model: An Activity Theoretical Approach to Artifact Ecologies. *Human-Computer Interaction*, 26(4), 315-371. DOI: 10.1080/07370024.2011.626709. 17, 80

Bødker, S. (2006) When Second Wave HCI meets Third Wave Challenges. In Proceedings of NordiCHI 2006 (pp. 1-8). New York: ACM. DOI: 10.1145/1182475.1182476. 30, 33, 60

Bødker, S. (1996) Creating conditions for participation: Conflicts and resources in systems design. *Human Computer Interaction*, 11(3), 215-236. DOI: 10.1207/s15327051hci1103_2.

Bødker, S., Ehn, P., Kammersgaard, J., Kyng, M., and Sundblad, Y. (1987) A Utopian experience: On design of Powerful Computer-based tools for skilled graphic workers. In G. Bjerknes, P. Ehn and M. Kyng. (Eds.), *Computers and Democracy: A Scandinavian Challenge* (pp. 251–278). Aldershot, UK: Avebury. 33

Chalmers, M. (2004) A Historical View of Context. *Computer Supported Cooperative Work*, 13, 223-247. DOI: 10.1007/s10606-004-2802-8. 29

Chen, B. X. (2010) *What the iPad Means for the Future of Computing.* Wired.com. 16

Chen, G. and Kotz, D. (2000) *A Survey of Context-Aware Mobile Computing Research.* (Paper TR2000-381). Department of Computer Science, Darthmouth College. 30

Cheverst, K., Davies, N., Mitchell, K., and Efstratiou, C. (2001) Using Context as a Crystal Ball: rewards and Pitfalls. *Personal and Ubiquitous Computing*, 5(1), 8-11. DOI: 10.1007/s007790170020. 30

Cheverst, K., Davies, N., Mitchell, K., Friday, A., and Efstratiou, C. (2000) Developing a Context-aware Electronic Tourist Guide: Some Issues and Experiences. In *Proceedings of CHI 2000*, The Hague, Amsterdam (pp. 17-24). New York: ACM. DOI: 10.1145/332040.332047. 30

Crabtree, B. and Rhodes, B. (1998) Wearable Computing and the Remembrance Agent. *BT Technology Journal*, 16(3), 118-124. DOI: 10.1023/A:1009642301754. 28, 30

Cross, N. (2011) *Design Thinking.* Oxford: Berg Publishers. 53, 54

Cross, N. (2001) Designerly ways of knowing: design discipline versus design science. *Design Issues*, 17(3), 49-55. DOI: 10.1162/074793601750357196. 48

Cross, N. (1999) Natural intelligence in design. *Design Studies*, 20, 25-39. DOI: 10.1016/S0142-694X(98)00026-X. 51, 53, 54

Cross, N. (1982) Designerly ways of knowing. *Design Studies*, 3(4), 221-227. DOI: 10.1016/0142-694X(82)90040-0. 48, 57

Dahlbom, B. and Mathiassen, L. (1993) *Computers in Context: The Philosophy and Practice of Systems Design*. Malden, MA: Blackwell Publishers Inc. 25, 45

Danis, C. and Karat, J. (1995) Technology-Driven Design of Speech Recognition Systems. In *Proceedings of the 1st Conference on Designing Interactive Systems: Processes, Practices, Methods, Techniques* (DIS '95), New York, USA (pp. 17-24). New York: ACM. DOI: 10.1145/225434.225437. 36

de Figueiredo, A. D. and da Cunha, P. R. (2007) Action Research and Design in Information Systems: Two Faces of a Single Coin. In N. Kock (Ed.), *Information Systems Action Research: An Applied View of Emerging Concepts and Methods* (pp. 61-95). New York: Springer. DOI: 10.1007/978-0-387-36060-7_4. 48, 49, 50, 51, 52, 53

de Sá, M. and Carrico, L. (2011) Designing and Evaluating Mobile Interaction: Challenges and Trends. *Foundations and Trends in Human Computer Interaction*, 4(3), 175-243. DOI: 10.1561/1100000025.

de Sá, M. and Carrico, L. (2009) A Mobile Tool for In-Situ Prototyping. In *Proceedings of MobileHCI 2009*, Bonn, Germany (article 20). New York: ACM. DOI: 10.1145/1613858.1613884. 29, 30

Design Research Society (1966) *First Statement of Rules, Inaugural Meeting of The Society*, 1966. 47

Dey, A. K. (2001) Understanding and Using Context. *Personal and Ubiquitous Computing*, 5(1), 4-7. DOI: 10.1007/s007790170019. 28, 29, 30

Dey, A. K. and Gregory, D. A (2000) Toward a better understanding of context and context-awareness. In *Proceedings of Workshop on the What, Who, Where, When and How of Context-Awareness*, CHI 2000.

Dix, A., Finlay, J., Abowd, G., and Beale, R. (2004) *Human-Computer Interaction* (3rd ed.). London: Prentice Hall Europe. 23

Dix, A., Rodden, T., Davies, N., Trevor, J., Friday, A., and Palfreyman, K. (2000) Exploiting Space and Location as a Design Framework for Interactive Mobile Systems. *ACM Transactions on Computer-Human Interaction* 7(3), 285-321. DOI: 10.1145/355324.355325. 30

Dourish, P. (2004) What we talk about when we talk about context. *Personal and Ubiquitous Computing*, 8(1), 19-30. DOI: 10.1007/s00779-003-0253-8. 28, 29

Dourish, P. (2001a) *Where the Action Is: The Foundations of Embodied Interaction*. Cambridge: The MIT Press.

Dourish, P. (2001b) Seeking a Foundation for Context-Aware Computing. *Human–Computer Interaction*, 16(2), 229-241. DOI: 10.1207/S15327051HCI16234_07. 29

Dreyfuss, H. (1955) *Designing for People* (2003 ed.). New York: Allworth Press. 33

Dubberly, H. and Evenson, S. (2011) Design as Learning—or "Knowledge Creation"—the SECI Model. *Interactions*, 18(1), 75-79. DOI: 10.1145/1897239.1897256. 71

Dubberly, H., Evenson, S., and Robinson, R. (2008) On modeling: The analysis-synthesis bridge model. *Interactions*, 15(2), 57-61. DOI: 10.1145/1340961.1340976. 71, 72

Edmonds, B. (1999) Pragmatic Holism (or pragmatic reductionism). *Foundations of Science*, 4(1), 57-82. DOI: 10.1023/A:1009642920187. 79, 80

Edwards, W. K. (2005) Putting Computing in Context: An Infrastructure to Support Extensible Context-Enhanced Collaborative Applications. *ACM Transactions On Computer–Human Interaction*, 12(4), 446-474. DOI: 10.1145/1121112.1121117. 30

Ehn, P. and Kyng, M. (1991) Cardboard Computers: Mocking-it-up or Hands-on the Future. In J. Greenbaum and M. Kyng (Eds.), *Design at Work* (pp. 169–196). Hillsdale, New Jersey: Laurence Erlbaum Associates Publishers. 33

Ehn, P. and Kyng, M. (1987) The Collective Resource Approach to Systems Design. In G. Bjerknes, P. Ehn and M. Kyng (Eds.), *Computers and Democracy: A Scandinavian Challenge* (pp. 251–278). Aldershot, UK: Avebury. 33

Erickson, T. (2006) Five Lenses: Toward a Toolkit for Interaction Design. In S. Bagnara and G. S. Smith (Eds.), *Theories and Practice in Interaction Design*. London: Lawrence Erlbaum Associates Publishers. 2

Einstein, A. (1931) *Cosmic Religion: With other Opinions and Aphorisms*. New York: Covici-Friede. 1

Fling, B. (2009) *Mobile Design and Development: Practical Concepts and Techniques for Creating Mobile Sites and Web Apps*. O'Reilly Media. 23

Fortunati, L. (2001) The Mobile Phone: An Identity on the move. *Personal and Ubiquitous Computing*, 5(2), 85-98. DOI: 10.1007/PL00000017. 29

Frederick, G. and Lal, R. (2010) *Beginning Smartphone Web Development: Building Javascript, CSS, HTML and Ajax-Based Applications for iPhone, Android, Palm Pre, Blackberry, Windows Mobile and Nokia S60*. Apress. 23

Gasson, S. (2006) *Emergence in Organizational Problem-solving: Theories of Social Cognition*. 49

Gasson, S. (2003) Human-Centered Vs. User-Centered Approaches to Information System Design. *Journal of Information Technology Theory and Application*, 5(2), 29-46. 64

Green, N., Harper, R. ,and Cooper, G. (2001) Configuring the Mobile User: Sociological and Industry Views. *Personal and Ubiquitous Computing*, 5(2), 146-156. DOI: 10.1007/s007790170017. 29

Greenbaum, J. and Mathiassen, L. (1990) Zen and the Art of Teaching Systems Development. *ACM Computers and Society*, 20(1), 26-30. DOI: 10.1145/379288.379293. 51

Greenfield, A. (2006) *Everyware: The Dawning Age of Ubiquitous Computing*. Berkeley: New Riders. 80

Gye, L. (2007) Picture This: the Impact of Mobile Camera Phones on Personal Photographic Practices- Continuum. *Journal of Media and Cultural Studies*, 21(2), 279-288. DOI: 10.1080/10304310701269107. 12

Hagen, P., Robertson, T., Kan, M., and Sadler, K. (2005) Emerging research methods for understanding mobile technology use. In *Proceedings of OZCHI 2005*, Canberra, Australia (pp. 1-10). New York: ACM. 30

Harman, G. H. (1965) The Inference to the Best Explanation. *Philosophical Review*, 74 (1), 88-95. DOI: 10.2307/2183532. 53

Harper, R., Rodden, T., Rogers, Y., and Sellen, A. (2008) *Being Human: Human-Computer Interaction in the year 2020*. Cambridge: Microsoft Research. 33, 59, 60

Harrison, S., Tatar, D., and Sengers, P. (2007) The three paradigms of HCI. In *Proceedings of CHI'07, alt.chi*. New York: ACM. 30

Helal, A., Haskell, B., Carter, J. L., Brice, R., Woelk, D.. and Rusinkiewich, M. (1999) *Any Time, Anywhere Computing: Mobile Computing Concepts aand Technology*. Boston, MA: Kluwer Academic Publishers. DOI: 10.1007/b115941. 23

Hinckley, K., Pierce, J., Sinclair, M., and Horvitz, E. (2000) Sensing techniques for mobile interaction. In *Proceedings of UIST 2000* (pp. 91-100). New York: ACM. DOI: 10.1145/354401.354417. 14

Hinckley, K. and Horvitz, E. (2001) Toward More Sensitive Mobile Phones. In *Proceedings of UIST 2001*, Orlando, Florida, USA (pp. 191-192). New York: ACM. DOI: 10.1145/502348.502382. 30

Hinckley, K., Pierce, J., Horvitz, E., and Sinclair, M. (2005) Foreground and background interaction with sensor-enhanced mobile devices. *ACM Transactions on Computer-Human Interaction*, 12(1), 31-52. DOI: 10.1145/1057237.1057240. 30

Hosbond, J. H. (2005) Mobile Systems Development: Challenges, Implications and Issues. In *Proceedings of MOBIS 2005*, Leeds, UK, IFIP TC8. DOI: 10.1007/0-387-31166-1_20. 29

Hutchins, E. (1995) *Cognition in the Wild*. Cambridge, MA: The MIT Press. 28

Höök, K. (2012) A Cry for More Tech at CHI!. *Interactions*, 19(2), 10-11. DOI: 10.1145/2090150.2090154. 37

IDEO (2009) *Human Centered Design Toolkit*, 2nd Edition. 71

Jameson, A. (2001) Modeling both the Context and the User. *Personal and Ubiquitous Computing*, 5(2), 29-33. DOI: 10.1007/s007790170025. 30

Jobs, S. (2011) *Apple Special Event*. San Francisco, 2 March, 2011. 25

Jobs, S. (2010) *Apple Announces iPad*. San Francisco, 27 January, 2010. 26, 37, 38

Johnson, P. (1998) Usability and Mobility; Interactions on the move. In *Proceedings of the First Workshop on Human-Computer Interaction with Mobile Devices*, Glasgow, Scotland (GIST Technical Report G98-1). 28

Jones, M. and Marsden, G. (2006) *Mobile Interaction Design*. Glasgow: John Wiley and Sons, Ltd. 21, 23, 25, 36

Jones, Q., Grandhi, S. A., Terveen, L., and Whittaker, S. (2004) People-to-People-to-Geographical-Places: The P3 Framework for Location-Based Community Systems. *Computer Supported Cooperative Work*, 13, 249-282. DOI: 10.1007/s10606-004-2803-7. 30

Jung, H., Stolterman, E., Ryan, W., Thompson, T., and Siegel, M. (2008) Toward a Framework for Ecologies of Artifacts: How Are Digital Artifacts Interconnected within a Personal Life? In *Proceedings of the 5th Nordic Conference on Human-Computer Interaction, NordiCHI 2008*, Lund, Sweden (pp 201-210). New York: ACM. DOI: 10.1145/1463160.1463182. 17, 80

Kaikkonen, A., Kekäläinen, A., Cankar, M., Kallio, T., and Kankainen, A. (2005) Usability Testing of Mobile Applications: A Comparison between Laboratory and Field Testing. *Journal of Usability Studies*, 1(1), 4-17. 30

Karapanos, E., Zimmerman, J., Forlizzi, J., and Martens, J. (2009) User Experience Over Time: An Initial Framework. In *Proceedings of CHI 2009*, Boston, MA, USA (pp. 729-738). New York: ACM. DOI: 10.1145/1518701.1518814. 30

Kay, Alan (1972). A Personal Computer for Children of All Ages. In *Proceedings of ACM National Conference*. Boston: New York: ACM. DOI: 10.1145/800193.1971922. 6

Kensing, F. and Blomberg, J. (1998) Participatory Design: Issues and Concerns. *Computer Supported Cooperative Work*, 7(1), 167–185. DOI: 10.1023/A:1008689307411. 33

Kindberg, T., Spasojevic M., Fleck R., and Sellen A. (2005) The Ubiquitous Camera: An In-Depth Study of Camera Phone Use. *IEEE Pervasive Computing*, 4(2), 42-50. DOI: 10.1109/MPRV.2005.42. 12

Kjeldskov, J. and Skov, M.B. (2014) Was it Worth the Hassle? Ten Years of Mobile HCI Research Discussions on Lab and Field Evaluations. In *Proceedings of Mobile HCI 2014*, Toronto, Canada. New York: ACM. 30

Kjeldskov, J. and Paay, J. (2012) A longitudinal review of mobile HCI research methods. A longitudinal review of Mobile HCI research Methods. In *Proceedings of Mobile HCI 2012*, San Francisco, USA (pp. 69-78). New York: ACM. DOI: 10.1145/2371574.2371586. 45

Kjeldskov, J., Skov, M. B., Nielsen, G. W., Thorup, S., and Vestergaard, M. (2013) Digital Urban Ambience: Mediating Context on Mobile Devices in the City. *Journal of Pervasive and Mobile Computing*. 19(5): 738-749. DOI: 10.1016/j.pmcj.2012.05.002. 30

Kjeldskov, J. and Stage, J. (2012) Combining ethnography and object-orientation: contextual richness and abstract models for mobile interaction design. *International Journal of Human-Computer Studies*, 70(3), 197–217. DOI: 10.1016/j.ijhcs.2011.10.004. 29

Kjeldskov, J. and Paay, J. (2010) Indexicality: understanding mobile human-computer interaction in context. *ACM Transactions on Computer-Human Interaction (TOCHI)*. 17(4). DOI: 10.1145/1879831.1879832. 30

Kjeldskov, J., Christensen, C. M., and Rasmussen, K. K. (2010) GeoHealth: a location-based service for home healthcare workers. *Journal of Location-Based Services*, 4(1), 3-27. DOI: 10.1080/17489721003742819. 30

Kjeldskov, J. and Skov, M. B. (2007) Exploring Context-Awareness for Ubiquitous Computing in the Healthcare Domain. *Personal and Ubiquitous Computing*, 11(7), 549-562. DOI: 10.1007/s00779-006-0112-5. 30

Kjeldskov, J., Graham, C., Pedell, S., Vetere, F., Howard, S., Balbo, S., and Davies, J. (2005) Evaluating the Usability of a Mobile Guide: The influence of Location, Participants and Resources. *Behaviour and Information Technology*, 24(1), 51-65. DOI: 10.1080/01449290512331319030. 30

Kjeldskov, J. and Paay, J. (2005) Just-for-Us: A Context-Aware Mobile Information System Facilitating Sociality. In *Proceedings of Mobile HCI 2005*, Salzburg, Austria (pp. 23-30). New York: ACM. DOI: 10.1145/1085777.1085782. 30

Kjeldskov, J., Skov, M. B., Als, B. S., and Høegh, R. T. (2004) Is it Worth the Hassle? Exploring the Added Value of Evaluating the Usability of Context-Aware Mobile Systems in the

Field. In *Proceedings of MobileHCI 2004*, Glasgow, Scotland, LNCS (pp. 61-73). Berlin: Springer-Verlag. DOI: 10.1007/978-3-540-28637-0_6. 30

Kjeldskov, J. and Howard, S. (2004) Envisioning Mobile Information Services: Combining User- and Technology-Centered Design. In *Proceedings of the 6th Asia-Pacific Conference on Human-Computer Interaction (APCHI 2004)*, Rotorua, New Zealand, LNCS (pp. 180-190). Berlin: Springer-Verlag. DOI: 10.1007/978-3-540-27795-8_19. 25

Kjeldskov, J. and Stage, J. (2004) New Techniques for Usability Evaluation of Mobile Systems. *International Journal of Human-Computer Studies*, 60(2004), 599-620. DOI: 10.1016/j.ijhcs.2003.11.001. 30

Kjeldskov, J. (2003) *Human-Computer Interaction Design for Emerging Technologies: Virtual Reality, Augmented Reality and Mobile Computer Systems*. Ph.D. Thesis, Department of Computer Science, Aalborg University, Denmark. ISSN 1601-0590 (no 23). 36

Kjeldskov, J. and Graham, C. (2003) A Review of MobileHCI Research Methods. In *Proceedings of the 5th International Mobile HCI 2003 Conference*, Udine, Italy, LNCS (pp. 317-335). Berlin: Springer-Verlag. DOI: 10.1007/978-3-540-45233-1_23. 36, 41

Kostakos, V., Nicolai, T., Yoneki, E., O'Neill, E., Kenn, H., and Crowcroft, J. (2009) Understanding and measuring the urban pervasive infrastructure. *Personal Ubiquitous Computing*, 13(5), 355-364. DOI: 10.1007/s00779-008-0196-1. 29

Köhler, W. (1947) *Gestalt Psychology: An Introduction to New Concepts in Modern Psychology*. New York: Liveright Publishing Corporation.

Lanzara, G. F. (1983) The design process: frames, metaphors and games. In U. Briefs, C. Ciborra, L. Schneider (Eds.), *Systems Design For, With and By The Users*. North-Holland Publishing Company. 48, 49, 50

Lauesen, S. (2005) *User Interface Design: A Software Engineering Perspective*. Harlow: Addison-Wesley. 23

Laurel, B. (Ed.) (1990) *The Art of Human-Computer Interface Design*. Reading, MA: Addison-Wesley. 23

Lewis, I. M. (1985) *Social Anthropology in Perspective*. Cambridge University Press.

Lindholm, C., Keinonen, T., and Kiljander, H. (2003) *Mobile Usability: How Nokia Changed the Face of the Mobile Phone*. New York: McGraw-Hill. 10, 23

Lindley, S. E., Harper, R., Randall, D., Glancy, M., and Smyth, N. (2009) Fixed in Time and "Time in Motion": Mobility of Vision through a SenseCam Lens. In *Proceedings of MobileHCI 2009*, Bonn, Germany (article 2). New York: ACM. DOI: 10.1145/1613858.1613861. 30

Ling, R. (2001) We Release Them Little by Little: Maturation and Gender Identity as Seen in the Use of Mobile Telephony. *Personal and Ubiquitous Computing*, 5(2), 123-136. DOI: 10.1007/s007790170015. 29

Little, L. and Briggs, P. (2009) Private whispers/public eyes: Is receiving highly personal information in a public place stressful? *Interacting with Computers*, 21(4), 316-322. DOI: 10.1016/j.intcom.2009.06.002. 30

Luff, P. and Heath, C. (1998) Mobility in Collaboration. In *Proceedings of CSCW'98*, Seattle, USA (pp. 305-314). New York: ACM. DOI: 10.1145/289444.289505. 29

Luther, K. and Diakopoulos, N. (2007) Distributed Creativity. In *Proceedings of Creativity and Cognition Workshop on Supporting Creative Acts Beyond Dissemination*, Washington, DC.

Lyons, K. and Starner, T. (2001) Mobile Capture for Wearable Computer Usability Testing. In *Proceedings of the 5th IEEE International Symposium on Wearable Computers*, Zurich, Switzerland. IEEE Press.

Martin, R. (2009) *The Design of Business: Why Design Thinking is the Next Competitive Advantage*. Harvard Business Press. 53, 54

McGillick, P. and Carlstrom, K. (2002) *Alex Popov: Buildings and Projects*. Axel Menges. 54, 55

Meggs, P. B. and Purvis, A. W. (2005) *Meggs' History of Graphic Design* (4th ed.). John Wiley and Sons.

McCullough, M. (2004) *Digital Ground—Architecture, Pervasive Computing, and Environmental Knowing*. Cambridge, MA: The MIT Press. 5, 28, 29

Mendel, J. and Yeager, J. (2010) Knowledge Visualization in Design Practice: Exploring the Power of Knowledge Visualization in Problem Solving. *Parsons Journal for Information Mapping*, 2(3), 1-4. 71

Mikkonen, M., Vayrynen, S., Ikonen, V., and Heikkila, O. (2002) User and Concept Studies as Tools in Developing Mobile Communication Services. *Personal and Ubiquitous Computing*, 2002(6), 113-124. DOI: 10.1007/s007790200010. 29

Miller, F. P., Vandome, A. F., and McBrewster, J. (2010) *Digital Ecosystem*. Alphascript Publishing. 17

Moggridge, B. (2007) *Designing Interactions*. Cambridge, MA: The MIT Press. 6, 7, 19, 24, 47, 57, 60, 63, 65, 66, 68

Moore, G., and Lottridge, D. (2010) Interaction design in the university: designing disciplinary interactions. In *CHI '10 Extended Abstracts*. ACM, New York, pp. 2735-2744. DOI: 10.1145/1753846.1753858. 24, 25

Murphy, J., Kjeldskov, J., Howard, S., Shanks, G., and Hartnell-Young, E. (2005) The Converged Appliance: "I Love it… But I Hate it." In *Proceedings of OzCHI 2005*, Canberra, Australia (pp. 1-10). New York: ACM. DOI: 10.1145/1108368.1108416. 12, 13, 14

Myers, M. D. (1997) Qualitative Research in Information Systems. *MIS Quarterly*, 21(2), 241-242. DOI: 10.2307/249422. 43

Nelson, H. G. and Stolterman, E. (2003) *The Design Way—Intentional Change in an Unpredictable World*. Englewood Cliffs, New Jersey: Educational Technology Publications. 49, 52, 55, 57

Nielsen, J. (2000) *WAP Field Study Findings*. Alertbox. 10

Nielsen, J. (1993) *Usability Engineering*. Boston: Academic Press. DOI: 10.1016/0306-4573(95)80026-P. 34

Nielsen, J. and Molich, R. (1990) Heuristic evaluation of user interfaces. In *Proceedings of CHI 1990*, Seattle, WA (pp. 249-256). New York: ACM. DOI: 10.1145/97243.97281. 34

Nonaka, I. and Toyama, R. (2002) A firm as a dialectical being: toward a dynamic theory of a firm. *Industrial and Corporate Change*, 11(5), 995-1009. DOI: 10.1093/icc/11.5.995. 25, 45

Norberg-Schulz, C. (1980) *Genius Loci: Toward a Phenomenology of Architecture*. New York: Rizzoli. 55

Norman, D. A. (2010) Technology First, Needs Last: The Research-Product Gulf. *Interactions*, 17(2), 38-42. DOI: 10.1145/1699775.1699784. 36, 38

Norman, D. A. (2005) Human-Centered Design Considered Harmful. *Interactions*, 12(4), 14-19. DOI: 10.1145/1070960.1070976. 62

Norman, D. A. (1998) *The Invisible Computer—Why Good Products Can Fail, the Personal Computer Is So Complex and Information Appliances Are the Solution*. Cambridge, MA: The MIT Press. 12

Norman, D. A. (1990) Four (more) issues for cognitive science. (Cognitive Science Technical Report No. 9001). Department of Cognitive Science, University of California, San Diego. 26

Norman, D. A. and Draper, S. W. (Eds.) (1986) *User Centered System Design: New Perspectives on Human-Computer Interaction*. Hillsdale: Lawrence Erlbaum Associates Publishers. 33

O'Hara, K., Kjeldskov, J., and Paay, J. (2011) Blended Interaction Spaces for Distributed Team Collaboration. *ACM Transactions on Computer-Human Interaction*, 18(1), article 3. DOI: 10.1145/1959022.1959025. 80

Olofsson, E. and Sjölén, K. (2005) *Design Sketching. Including an Extensive Collection of Inspiring Sketches by 24 Students at the Umeå Institute of Design* (2nd ed.). Klippan: Ljungbergs Tryckeri.

Oulasvirta, A. (2009) Field Experiments in HCI: Promises and Challenges. In P. Saariluoma and H. Isomaki (Eds.), *Future Interaction Design II*. Berlin: Springer-Verlag. DOI: 10.1007/978-1-84800-385-9_5. 30

Oulasvirta, A. and Nyyssonen, T. (2009) Flexible hardware configurations for studying mobile usability. *Journal of Usability Studies*, 4(2), 93-105. 30

Paay, J., Kjeldskov, J., Howard S.. and Dave, B. (2009b) Out on the town: a socio-physical approach to the design of a context aware urban guide. *Transactions on Computer-Human Interaction*, 16(2), 7-34. DOI: 10.1145/1534903.1534904.

Paay, J., Sterling, L., Vetere, F., Howard, S., and Boettcher, A. (2009a) Engineering the social: The role of shared artifacts. *International Journal of Human-Computer Studies*, 67(5), 437-454. DOI: 10.1016/j.ijhcs.2008.12.002. 29

Paay, J., (2008) From ethnography to interface design. In J. Lumsden (Ed.), *Handbook of Research on User Interface Design and Evaluation for Mobile Technology* (pp. 1-15). PA, USA: Idea Group Inc (IGI). DOI: 10.4018/978-1-59904-871-0.ch001. 29

Paay, J. and Kjeldskov, J. (2008b) Understanding the user experience of location based services: five principles of perceptual organization applied. *Journal of Location-Based Services*, 2(4), 267-286. DOI: 10.1080/17489720802609328. 30

Paay, J. and Kjeldskov, J. (2008a) Situated Social Interactions: a Case Study of Public Places in the City. *Computer-Supported Cooperative Work*, 17(2-3), 275-290. DOI: 10.1007/s10606-007-9072-1. 29

Paay, J. and Kjeldskov, J. (2005) Understanding and Modelling the Built Environment for Mobile Guide Interface Design. *Behaviour and Information Technology*, 24(1), 21-35. DOI: 10.1080/01449290512331319012. 29

Palen, L., Salzman, M., and Youngs, E. (2000) Going Wireless: Behavior & Practice of New Mobile Phone Users. In *Proceedings of CSCW 2000*, Philadelphia, PA, USA (pp. 201-210). New York: ACM. DOI: 10.1145/358916.358991. 30

Peirce, C. S. (1931-58) Collected Writings (8 Vols.). In C. Hartshorne, P. Weiss, and A. Burks (Eds.), *Collected Papers of Charles Sanders Peirce*. Cambridge, MA: Harvard University Press. 53

Pepper, S. C. (1942) *World Hypothesis: A Study in Evidence*. Berkeley: University of California Press. 51, 53

Perry, M., O'Hara, K., Sellen, A., Brown, B., and Harper, R. (2001) Dealing with mobility: understanding access anytime, anywhere. *ACM Transactions on Computer-Human Interaction*, 8(4), 323-347. DOI: 10.1145/504704.504707. 29

Preece, J., Rogers, Y., and Sharp H. (2002) *Interaction Design: beyond Human-Computer Interaction*. New York: John Wiley and Sons Ltd. DOI: 10.1145/512526.512528. 23, 33

Preece, J., Rogers, Y., Sharp, H., Benyon, D., Holland, S., and Carey, T. (1994) *Human-Computer Interaction*. Workingham: Addison-Wesley. 23

Preece, J., Benyon, D., Davies, G., Keller, L., and Rogers, Y. (1993) *A Guide to Usability: Human Factors in Computing*. Harlow: Addison-Wesley. 34

Raman, V. V. (2005) Scientific Reductionism and Holism: Two Sides of the Perception of Reality. *Theology and Science*, 3(3), 250-253. DOI: 10.1080/14746700500317230. 79, 80

Ramsay, M. and Nielsen, J. (2000) *WAP Usability: Déjà Vu: 1994 All Over Again*. (Nielsen Norman Group Report, December 2000). 10

Rapoport, R. N. (1970) Three Dilemmas in Action Research. *Human Relations*, 23(4), 499-513. DOI: 10.1177/001872677002300601.

Raskin, J. (2000) *The Humane Interface: New Directions for Interactive Systems*. Boston: Addison-Wesley. 23

Rasmussen, L. B. (2007) From human-centered to human-context centered approach: looking back over 'the hills', what has been gained and lost? *AI & Society*, 2007(21), 471-495. DOI: 10.1007/s00146-007-0088-3. 25, 45, 64

Ray, K. (1980) *Contextual Architecture: Responding to Existing Style*. New York: McGraw-Hill. 54

Reichl, P., Frohlich P., Baillie L., Schatz R., and Dantcheva A. (2007) The LiLiPUT Prototype: A Wearable Lab Environment for User Tests of Mobile Telecommunication Applications. *CHI 2007 Extended Abstracts*, San Jose, California, USA (pp. 1833-1838). New York: ACM. DOI: 10.1145/1240866.1240907. 30

Rittel H. W. J. and Webber M. M. (1973) Dilemmas in a General Theory of Planning. *Policy Sciences*, 4(2), 155-196. DOI: 10.1007/BF01405730. 52

Robertson, T. (1997) Cooperative Work and Lived Cognition: A Taxonomy of Embodied Actions. In *Proceedings of ECSCW 1997*, (pp. 205-220). DOI: 10.1007/978-94-015-7372-6_14.

Rodden, T., Cheverst, K., Davies, N.. and Dix, A. (1998) Exploiting Context in HCI Design for Mobile Systems. In *Proceedings of the First Workshop on Human-Computer Interaction with Mobile Devices*, Glasgow, Scotland (GIST Technical Report G98-1). DOI: 10.1.1.57.1279. 28

Rogers, Y., Sharp, H., and Preece, J. (2011) *Interaction Design: Beyond Human-Computer Interaction* (3rd ed.). New York: John Wiley and Sons Ltd. 23

Rogers, Y., Connelly, K., Tedesco, L., Hazlewood, W., Kurtz, A., Hall, R. E., Hursey, J., and Toscos, T. (2007) Why it's worth the hassle: the value of in-situ studies when designing Ubicomp. In *Proceedings UbiComp 2007*, LNCS (pp. 336-353). Berlin: Springer-Verlag. DOI: 10.1007/978-3-540-74853-3_20. 30

Rogers, Y., Scaife M., and Rizzo, A. (2005) Interdisciplinarity: an Emergent or Engineered Process. In S. J. Derry, C. D. Schunn and M. A. Gernsbacher (Eds.), *Interdisciplinary Collaboration*. Mahwah, New Jersey: LEA. 24, 25, 26, 27, 46

Rogers, Y. (2004) New theoretical approaches for human-computer interaction. *Annual review of Information Science and Technology (ARIST)*, 38, 87-143. DOI: 10.1.1.102.8355. 47

Rogers, Y., Scaife, M., Harris, E., Phelps, T., Price, S., Smith, H., Muller, H., Randell, C., Moss, A., Taylor, I., Stanton, D., O'Malley, C., Corke, G., and Gabrielli, S. (2002) Things aren't what they seem to be: innovation through technology inspiration. In *Proceedings of the 4th conference on Designing interactive systems: processes, practices, methods, and techniques (DIS 2002)*(pp. 373-378). New York: ACM. DOI: 10.1145/778712.778766. 36

Rosson, M. B. and Carroll, J. M. (2001) *Usability Engineering: Scenario-Based Development of Human-Computer Interaction*. San Francisco, CA: Morgan Kaufmann Publishers. 34

Rowland, D., Flintham, M., Oppermann, L. Marshall, J., Chamberlain, A., Koleva, B., Benford, S. and Peres, C. (2009) Ubikequitous Computing: Designing Interactive Experiences for Cyclists. In *Proceedings of MobileHCI 2009*, Bonn, Germany (article 21). New York: ACM. DOI: 10.1145/1613858.1613886. 30

Rubin, J. (1994) *Handbook of Usability Testing: How To Plan, Design, and Conduct Effective Tests*. New York: John Wiley and Sons Ltd. 34

Saffer, D. (2007) *Designing for Interaction: Creating Smart Applications and Clever Devices*. Berkeley, CA: AIGA Design Press/New Riders. 62

Schmidt, A., Aidoo, K. A., Takaluoma, A., Tuomela, U., Van Laerhoven, K. and Van de Velde, W. (1999b) Advanced Interaction in Context. In *Proceedings of HUC 1999* (pp. 89-101). London: Springer-Verlag. DOI: 10.1007/3-540-48157-5_10. 30

Schmidt, A., Beigl, M., and Gellersen, H. (1999a) There is more to Context than Location. *Computers and Graphics Journal*, 23(6), 893-902. DOI: 10.1016/S0097-8493(99)00120-X. 28, 30

Schilit, B. and Theimer, M. (1994) Disseminating active map information to mobile hosts. *IEEE Network*, 8(5), 22-32. DOI: 10.1109/65.313011. 28, 30

Schön, D. A. (1983) *The Reflective Practitioner: How Professionals Think in Action*. New York: Basic Books. 48, 49, 50, 51, 54

Schön, D. A. (1992) Designing as reflective conversation with the materials of a design situation. *Research and Engineering Design*, 3(3), 131-147. DOI: 10.1007/BF01580516. 49, 50

Shane, G. (1976) Contextualism. *Architectural Design*, 46(11), 676-679. 54

Sharp, H., Rogers, Y., and Preece, J. (2007) *Interaction Design: Beyond Human-Computer Interaction* (2nd ed.). Barcelona: John Wiley and Sons Ltd. 19, 20, 21, 24, 33

Sharples, M., Corlett, D. and Westmancott, O. (2002) The Design and Implementation of a Mobile Learning Resource. *Personal and Ubiquitous Computing*, 2002(6), 220-234. DOI: 10.1007/s007790200021. 29

Shneiderman, B. (1998) *Designing the User interface: Strategies for Effective Human-Computer Interaction* (3rd ed.). Workingham: Addison-Wesley. 23

Simon, H. A. (1969) *The Sciences of the Artificial*. Cambridge, MA: The MIT Press. 48, 49, 50, 51

Simon, H. A. (1962) The Architecture of Complexity. *Proceedings of the American Philosophical Society*, 106(6), 467-482. 80

Skov, M. B., Kjeldskov, J., Paay, J., Husted, N., Nørskov, J., and Pedersen, K. (2013) Designing on-site: Facilitating Participatory Contextual Architecture with Mobile Phone. *Journal of Pervasive and Mobile Computing*. 19(2): 216-227. DOI: 10.1016/j.pmcj.2012.05.004.

Smith, G. C. (2007) *What in Interaction Design? In B. Moggridge (2007) Designing Interactions*. Cambridge, MA: The MIT Press. 20

Snyder, C. (2003) *Paper Prototyping: The Fast and Easy Way To Design and Refine User Interfaces*. Amsterdam: Morgan Kaufmann Publishers.

Spool, J. M., Scanlon, T., Schroeder, W., Snyder, C., and DeAngelo, T. (1999) *Web Site Usability: A Designers Guide*. San Francisco: Morgan Kaufmann Publishers. 34

Star, S. L. and Griesemer, J. R. (1989) Institutional Ecology, 'Translations' and Boundary Objects: Amateurs and Professionals in Berkeley's Museum of Vertebrate Zoology, 1907-39. *Social Studies of Science*, 19, 387-420. DOI: 10.1177/030631289019003001. 29

Stokholm, M. (2010) *Stepping Stones I - En Model for Integrering Af Proces Elementer*. Unpublished working paper. 65

Stokholm, M. (2008) A Holistic Approach to Interdisciplinary Innovation Supported by a Simple Tool. In *Proceedings of the 9th International Conference on Human Factors in Organizational Design and Management* (pp. 143-149). Santa Monica: IEA Press. 65

Stolterman, E. (2008) The nature of design practice and implications for interaction design research. *International Journal of Design*, 2(1), 55-65. 47, 52

Sørensen, H., Raptis, D., Kjeldskov, J.,, and Skov, M.B. (2014) The DIWiDE Framework: Principles of Interaction in Digital Ecosystems. In *Proceedings of UbiComp 2014*, Seattle, USA. New York: ACM. 17, 80

The Royal Society (1996) *Interdisciplinarity—Transport and the Environment*. 26, 27

Tufte E. R. (2001) *The Visual Display of Quantitative Information* (2nd ed.). Cheshire, Connecticut: Graphics Press.

Tufte, E. R. (1997) *Visual Explanations: Images and Quantities, Evidence and Narrative*. Cheshire, Connecticut: Graphics Press.

Tufte, E. R. (1990) *Envisioning Information*. Cheshire, Connecticut: Graphics Press. DOI: 10.1002/aic.690390220.

Turner, J. A. (1987) Understanding The Elements Of Systems Design. In R. J. Boland and R. A. Hirschheim (Eds.), Critical Issues In *Information Systems Research*. John Wiley and Sons Ltd.

van den Ende, J. and Dolfsma, W. (2004) Technology-push, demand-pull and the shaping of technological paradigms: Patterns in the development of computing technology. *Journal of Evolutionary Economics*, 15(1), 83-99. DOI: 10.1007/s00191-004-0220-1. 36

Verganti, R. (2010) Apple's Secret? It Tells Us What We Should Love. 37, 38

Verganti, R. (2009) *Design-Driven Innovation: Changing the Rules of Competition by Radically Innovating What Things Mean*. Boston: Harvard Business Press. 38

Vetere, F., Gibbs, M., Kjeldskov, J., Howard, S., Mueller, F., Pedell, S., Mecoles, K., and Bunyan, M. (2005) Mediating Intimacy: Designing Technologies to Support Strong-Tie Relationships. In *Proceedings of CHI 2005*, Portland, Oregon, USA (pp. 471-480). New York: ACM. DOI: 10.1145/1054972.1055038.

Viller, S. and Sommerville, I. (2000) Ethnographically informed analysis for software engineers. *International Journal of Human–Computer Studies*, 53, 169-196. DOI: 10.1006/ijhc.2000.0370.

Weilenmann, A. (2001) Negotiating Use: Making Sense of Mobile Technology. *Personal and Ubiquitous Computing*, 5(2), 137-145. DOI: 10.1007/PL00000015. 30

Weiser, M. (1991) The Computer for the 21st Century. *Scientific American*, 265(3), 94-104. DOI: 10.1038/scientificamerican0991-94. 5

Weiss, S. (2002) *Handheld Usability*. Milan: John Wiley and Sons Ltd. DOI: 10.1145/778712.778775. 23, 34

Wilde, O. (1889) *The Decay of Lying*. Penguin Classics. 10

Winograd, T. (1997) The Design of Interaction (aka. From Computing Machinery to interaction design). In P. Denning and R. Metcalfe (Eds.), *Beyond Calculation: The Next Fifty Years of Computing*. Amsterdam: Springer-Verlag.

Winograd, T. (1996) *Bringing Design to Software*. Reading, MA: Addison-Wesley. 19, 23, 49

Wynekoop, J. L. and Conger, S. A. (1990) A Review of Computer Aided Software Engineering Research Methods. In *Proceedings of the IFIP TC8 WG 8.2 Working Conference on The Information Systems Research Arena of The 90's*, Copenhagen, Denmark. 40, 43

Yin, R. K. (1994) *Case Study Research, Design and Methods* (2nd ed.). Newbury Park: Sage Publications.

Zuberec, S. (2000) The interaction design of Microsoft Windows CE. In E. Bergman (Ed.), *Information Appliances and Beyond*. San Francisco: Morgan Kaufmann Publishers. 16

Author Biography

Jesper Kjeldskov, Dr. Scient., Ph.D. is Professor of Computer Science at Aalborg University in Denmark within the area of Human-Computer Interaction, and research leader in the newly established Research Centre for Socio+Interactive Design. Jesper's research interests are Interaction Design and User Experience with particular focus on mobile and ubiquitous technologies primarily in non-work settings. Jesper has a cross-disciplinary background spanning the humanities, social sciences, and computer science. He has published more than 130 peer-reviewed journal and conference papers within the area of Human-Computer Interaction. In 2013 he was awarded the degree of Doctor of Science (higher doctorate) and subsequently promoted to Full Professor. Prior to his professorship at Aalborg, Jesper lived and worked for several years in Australia, working as a Research Fellow at The University of Melbourne, and as a Principal Research Scientist at CSIRO in Sydney. Since 2009 he has revisited his interests in mobile HCI and has extended his work on domestic computing with new projects within sustainability, digital media, mediated relationships, emerging display technologies, and social natural user interfaces. In his spare time Jesper loves food, wine, music, and having a laugh with his partner-in-crime, Jeni Paay.

Printed in the United States
by Baker & Taylor Publisher Services